MOUNTIE MAKERS
Putting the
CANADIAN
in RCMP

Copyright © 1997 Robert Gordon Teather
First Heritage House edition, 1997 (ISBN 1-895811-41-4)
Second edition, 2004

Library and Archives Canada Cataloguing in Publication

Teather, Robert Gordon, 1947-
    Mountie Makers, putting the Canadian in RCMP/
    Robert Gordon Teather. — 2nd ed.

ISBN 1-894384-79-2

    1. Teather, Robert Gordon, 1947-   2. Police training—Canada.
3. Royal Canadian Mounted Police—Biography. I. Title

HV8158.5.T42 2004   363.2'092   C2004-904732-9

Heritage House acknowledges the financial support for our publishing
program from the Government of Canada through the Book Publishing
Industry Development Program (BPIDP), Canada Council for the Arts, and
the British Columbia Arts Council.

Cover design: Nancy St. Gelais
Book design: Catherine Mack
Editor: Rhonda Bailey
Front cover photo: R.G. Teather
Back cover photos: R. David O'Brien (top), Vancouver *Province* (author)
Additional photos: Const. Guy Dewolf, pages 9, 13, 42, 47, 105, 115, 140, 157;
Const. Bruce Hamilton, pages 17, 65, 86, 97; Gary Haney, page 127; R. David
O'Brien, pages 29, 149, 151; RCMP Museum (Depot), pages 59, 72, 156.

HERITAGE HOUSE PUBLISHING COMPANY LTD.
Unit #108 – 17665 66A Ave., Surrey, BC V3S 2A7

Printed in Canada

BRITISH
COLUMBIA
ARTS COUNCIL
We acknowledge the support of the Province of British Columbia
through the British Columbia Arts Council

The Canada Council | Le Conseil des Arts
for the Arts | du Canada

DEDICATION

To my father, who never said goodbye; to Ben, who did; to my dear friends Len Krygsveld, Elsa McElroy, and Bill Heckler; to Janice Peace, who made the completion of this book po ssible; and to my warm, caring, and loving wife, Susan, whom I will always love dearly.

CONTENTS

Introduction

"You have arrived here today as a troop of individuals, but you will leave this academy as an individual troop or not at all!" The words shouted at us by our Corps Sergeant Major, and repeated often by our Drill Corporal, still ring clearly in my ears after serving with the Royal Canadian Mounted Police for twenty-nine years. Those were the first words we heard as new recruits to the RCMP. Those were the words that ensured our survival through six months of basic recruit training. We learned that by combining our strengths and adopting a common goal, we could acquire a degree of strength and courage as a team that we did not have as individuals.

The training techniques of the RCMP have historically been shrouded in secrecy. The public has been given only glimpses of this secret protocol during tightly controlled visits to the RCMP Training Academy in Regina, Saskatchewan, and in sporadic television documentaries and written articles. Torturous instruction techniques and brain-moulding (some would call it brain-washing) forces are applied to new members of Canada's national police force during their training. Until now they have remained confidential, spoken of solely by members of our Force while reminiscing during the wee hours of the morning.

Such memories have rarely been shared with wives or close friends, let alone the general public. Should you ever be sitting with a Mountie when the hour is late and a look of longing overtakes his face, I recommend silence. If his mouth should speak the phrase, "I can still remember when … ," then sit back and listen. You are about to be let into a very exclusive club—a club so tight-knit that until now the doors have been locked and the shutters drawn.

When I wrote *Scarlet Tunic, Volumes I* and *II*, I confessed to revealing many secrets of the RCMP, and I feared retribution from our Force. Understandably, the response from "Upper Management" has been silence, but my peers across Canada have responded with telephone calls and letters.

That support has encouraged me to disclose more of our secrets, strengths, and weaknesses. It is important to all of us that you understand who we are and what we do, and that we consider ourselves no better and no worse than you are.

But we are different. Very different.

We have been made different through the RCMP training procedure. To outsiders, this process may appear brutal and tough throughout, but it has worked for over one hundred years. Times have changed, and it is a shame indeed that the training historically used to "make Mounties" is now being tempered—some would say corrupted—by pop psychology and the confused priorities of the Me Generation. All is not lost, however. Today's Mounties still encounter veteran trainers more than willing to pass on the traditions, but the relationship has changed. Today, a new arrival into the RCMP training academy is not a sworn member of the Force. As cadets, they complete the six months' basic training, and only upon graduation can they apply for membership in the Royal Canadian Mounted Police.

Not all are accepted.

I would be shirking my duty and my promise of truth to you if I did not insert this paragraph. In the past six months, I have befriended an RCMP Cadet who, as I write this book, is currently undergoing his basic training—training that employs methods very different than those described in this book. Cadet, not Constable, is the new title our Force gives its recruits. During our time together, I have learned that some of the training traditions, at least the important ones, are still maintained. My young "brother-in-law" embraces the new loyalties he has developed, both toward his RCMP comrades in training and for the country he has chosen to serve. The stories of his troop, of their closeness and of their pulling together during the toughest of times, make me add to this introduction a toast. "Here's to you, Cadet, soon-to-be Constable, Guy Dewolf. I know where you have been and I know where it will lead you. I salute you and your troop, Troop 14."

Even today, the words of Corporal Don Withers, my mentor, instructor, and dear friend, are held to be true. "You must be strong in order to be gentle and you must be brutal in order to be kind. You will learn to be strong and brutal or you will not survive."

This is our story, the story of my Troop 18—in 1967 at Depot in Regina, Saskatchewan—and how we learn strength and brutality so that we might serve a police force known internationally for its gentleness and kindness.

As with my other books, this story is not really about me, nor is it just about my troop. It represents all the troops who have graduated from the RCMP training programs in the past 124 years.

It is about the brutal and tough, the gentle and kind police officers who have sworn to *"Maintiens le Droit*—Maintain the Right."

In writing this book, I salute the men I trained with—Troop 18. I salute their trust, their camaraderie, and the loyalty of all my fellow police officers—those living and those who have now passed on to a greater world.

The events described within are fact; however, certain liberties have been taken. The tales you are about to read occurred over a six-month period. They involved members of three different troops undergoing Royal Canadian Mounted Police (RCMP) Basic Recruit Training. The police officers are real people with whom I have shared blood, sweat, tears, laughter, pain, and cold showers.

I have also shared a bond of trust and undying friendship with these people. For this reason I have changed their names within the text, thus granting them the choice of keeping their anonymity or proudly proclaiming "Yeah, those were the good ol' days!"

We live in an era where Canadians are struggling with issues related to national unity, such as the concept of "distinct societies" within Canada. This story addresses such issues through the magical hell of RCMP boot camp as young men are brought together from across our vast country and given a common purpose. They cease to be BCers, Albertans, or Ontarians. Through a unique and heretofore secret training, they shed their regionalism and accept the confines of a common mould. They are not only shaped into Mounties, they also become Canadians.

Here are my brothers at a point in time when all our lives were changed forever. Prairie Dog, from Saskatchewan; Lumchuck, from Alberta; Didarski, who brought with him from Nova Scotia one ear larger than the other; the nomadic and mysterious André Byrant, whose past is cloaked in secrecy; and the hero of this story, Francois Labeau, whose reputation for courage and determination still lives on in the hearts of his troopmates, even after thirty years. Francois, a young, spirited Québécois, will tug at your heart as you learn the truth behind the making of a Mountie.

I hope that you can read this book in a quiet retreat where you can open your heart and accept our humanity as I invite you into a world where few have gone before.

Welcome to Regina, Saskatchewan, RCMP Depot Division, birthing centre for Mounties. Welcome to the frozen Prairie where I first learned what being Canadian was all about.

Welcome to hell.

"When I left my home and family, I was no more than a boy ... running scared."

Paul Simon ("The Boxer")

CHAPTER ONE
Departure—Fear, Vomit, and Four Quarts of Oil

Sunday, September 10: The alarm clock tore its way into my dreams, drew me back to reality, and signalled the beginning of another day. The first day of my six-month journey to a new life.

Reluctantly at first, I wiped the sleep-crusties from my eyes, chewed my tongue and left my dreams behind. Today was different and I knew it. It was a day like none I had ever experienced. I was only twenty years old, and although I had sought the freedom of leaving home, I feared today's arrival. As my thoughts took shape inside my head, my stomach cramped. Fear, anticipation, sadness, and uncertainty all gathered to make their presence known. Yesterday I had been "sworn in." I was now officially a member of the Royal Canadian Mounted Police. My life was no longer my own. Today I would leave home, drive fifteen hundred miles from Hamilton, Ontario, to Regina, Saskatchewan, and begin six months' training—training so rigid that because of the insults and injuries received during this time many did not graduate. On occasion, the brutal training took the ultimate toll, and a recruit would lose his life. The great mystery of the RCMP moulding process lay ahead of me, and I could feel only fear. Like most people, I knew nothing of the training. It would be many years before I realized that if you listened closely to veterans of the RCMP, if you listened very, very closely to late-night confessions or casual reflections, you might hear now and then, between the tales they spun, a short reference to a comrade who was sent home wounded, crippled—or even worse—dead. It was a secret well kept that not all recruits would survive training.

My mind was already heading west when something brought me back to full awareness of my surroundings. I was not alone in my bedroom. I could feel a presence—the weight of someone sitting at the foot of my bed.

"Good morning, son."

"G'morning," I replied, looking up from my pillow.

"Well, I suppose this is it."

"Uh huh." I muttered the words, still half-asleep. Then my father spoke the three words I would never forget.

"No hard feelings?"

For years my relationship with my father had been quite stormy, and my joining the Royal Canadian Mounted Police had a dual purpose. It would allow me both to escape from home and to prove my worth as an adult, although I was unsure of what it meant to be an adult.

"No," I answered. "No hard feelings, Dad."

"That's good." His voice cracked. It was still dark, but a sliver of kitchen light that shone in through the partially open bedroom door defined his silhouette. His head was bowed and he was motionless. He placed his hand gently on my leg, and through the covers, gave it a squeeze. "Then I guess you had better get rustling. You've a long journey ahead of you."

"Yeah, I suppose so." I threw back the covers and swung my legs down until my feet hit the floor.

"I ... just wanted to say ... " Dad's words stopped short.

"Yes?" I looked at my father, but his eyes did not meet mine.

There was another pause. "Never mind," he finally said as he rose from the bed and walked into the kitchen. I would never know what it was he could not say, but the memory of those unspoken words still haunts me. Sentences between father and son should never be cut short, and questions should never go unanswered.

It was 4:00 a.m. and in a short thirty minutes I would leave home. Forever. After a quick orange juice and one last slice of my mother's homemade toast, I gave a brief goodbye to my parents and headed out the door toward my car. Hiding both fear and sadness, I was unable to admit to myself that I was running away.

I climbed into the 1958 Dodge that my dad had made roadworthy for the three-day journey that lay ahead. The ignition key turned easily, and the engine belched one small puff of blue smoke from the exhaust pipe. Hanging from the dash-mounted rearview mirror was a handwritten note my father had penned: "Don't forget! One quart of oil every four hundred miles!!!"

The three exclamation marks told me this was important. As I backed out of the driveway, I could see my parents, holding each other and waving goodbye. My eyes filled with tears as I returned their wave, but I refused to let them see my emotions. For twenty years I had managed to keep my feelings locked away. My father had taught me well.

It was years later that I learned the whole story of the day I left home. Dad, it seems, returned home from work, only a few short hours into his shift. He had come home to drink coffee—and to weep.

And yet he had never let me know how he felt.

Pushing down on the accelerator I took one last look over my shoulder, not sure if I would ever see my house again. I came to a full stop at the end of my street and turned left. Youth's journey had ended and another had begun.

A half-mile down the road the weight of my decision pressed down on my twenty-year-old brain. I had left home. Forever. Somewhere on the Canadian Prairie, the Royal Canadian Mounted Police training academy awaited my arrival. They had given me a number, 26112, and a title—Constable. I had reluctantly accepted their invitation—a decision I would soon regret.

DRILL HALL

Had I known what had awaited, I might never have left home. The drill hall will always live in the memory of all who strove to become "an individual troop." It was a place where feet became sore, discipline became commonplace, and boys became men.

I had grown up, and "putting away all childish things" meant that I would be saying goodbye to everything I had known to be good, comfortable, and secure. Without warning, a knot tightened in my stomach, and I jerked the car to the side of the road, threw open the door, and leaned out as far as I could.

Looking down at the gravel, I watched a pool of vomit form on the asphalt—eight ounces of orange juice and Mom's toasted homemade bread.

That was merely the beginning. I retched again. I retched so hard my eyes bled, my toes curled, and my teeth chattered. As my stomach continued to launch its contents onto the gravel shoulder, I prayed for deliverance from this cowardly act. The contractions lessened, and I watched as the pool of vomit slowly moved away. Then I noticed that in my moment of weakness I had forgotten to take the car out of gear, and it had crept forward until it had been not-so-gently stopped by a telephone pole.

"Great! Just bloody great!" I groaned. I climbed out of the car, stepped over my toast and orange juice, and inspected the damage. It was barely noticeable. "Great way to begin a new life," I said out loud. It was 4:40 a.m. and there were no witnesses to my brief soliloquy. Climbing back into my car, I realized a new sense of loneliness.

It was a strange experience, this growing up. It tasted like vomit, looked like a dented car, and rattled like four quarts of oil on the back floor of a 1958 Dodge.

Following the dusty trail of all my childhood cowboy heroes, I climbed back onto my makeshift saddle and drove off into the west.

"I never think of the future. It comes soon enough."
                                                    Albert Einstein

CHAPTER TWO
The Arrival—Introduction to Hell

Wednesday, September 13: It was a long drive from Hamilton to Regina. A fifteen-hundred-mile drive, punctuated with two flat tires, four quarts of oil, and endless hours behind the steering wheel of a red and white 1958 Dodge. Countless times I glanced at the many notes my father had taped to the dashboard and the rearview mirror.

"Add oil every four hundred miles." I had obeyed that command.

"Do not ride the brakes. They should last you to Regina." That was comforting.

"Do not drive over fifty miles per hour. She's an old car." More comforting thoughts.

"When cold-starting the engine, remove the air filter and wedge open the carburettor butterfly valve with the stick located under front seat." Only once was that reminder necessary. Mostly I drove until my eyelids grew heavy. Then for a few hours I slept, curled up on the bench seat. Awake again, I drove steadily until another quart of oil was needed.

Highways 401 and 7 North and my family home soon became a distant memory as Highway 1 guided me west.

Endless bags of potato chips and cola combined with tire pressure checks (two between each quart of oil—I obeyed that note also) and the continuous curves in the road were my main focus as I drove along the north shores of lakes Huron and Superior. My only pause on the three-day journey was a brief visit to Stonewall, Manitoba. My sister and brother-in-law had invited me to stop over for a meal and a real bed. Accepting their invitation, I ate like a pig and enjoyed the last soft mattress I would experience for six months.

The following morning saw a quick goodbye: a kiss from my sister and a firm handshake from my brother-in-law. He had been a member of the Force for nearly three years and already knew all there was to know about law enforcement.

That's what he told me.

I used Dad's piece of wood on the carburettor, threw it under the front seat, and quickly replaced the air filter. Waving goodbye to two friends, I drove west, once again following the path of my childhood cowboys.

The roads in Manitoba were insane—but not as insane as they were in Saskatchewan. Crossing the border into Saskatchewan, I discovered the essence of the word "flat." Other words could be used to describe Saskatchewan's roads—words like "level," "prostrate," "bleak," and even "hopeless"—but "flat" still remains in my mind as the only word that is truly worthy of an endless stretch of highway with no turns, no gradient, no diversity, and no end.

But my road did indeed have an end, and it was posted in green letters on a white background: Regina 10 miles.

I pulled my car over to collect my thoughts. I was long beyond the point of no return. I had run out of money, but more important, I had run out of oil. Less than fifty dollars remained in my pocket. Enough for the next ten miles, to be sure. All I would need for the next six months would be provided by the Royal Canadian Mounted Police. The RCMP would afford me room, board, and a six-month regimen of discipline.

Fifteen minutes past Regina's road sign, I pulled into Depot Division. Many times since I decided to enlist, I had wondered how a police training division had acquired such a funny name. On one occasion, I explored the hidden reaches of an old dictionary where I read: " Depot, n. place for stores."

Either I had arrived at a shopping centre or a place where I would be stored, for what purpose I could not imagine.

Depot was not a shopping centre.

My car sputtered a short fifteen-hundred-mile thank you as I turned off its engine. Parking in a bleak, near-empty lot I climbed out, stretched my body, and closed the car door.

"Who the bloody hell are you and where's your tie? I thought I told you to get a haircut, lad. What the hell is your name anyway? Can you hear me? Don't just stand there like a useless lump of shit. I asked you a question."

Paralyzed, I stood still as the assault continued.

"I asked you a question. Are you deaf or just stupid?"

Proving I was not deaf, I attempted an answer. "Could you please tell me where I ... "

"I'll tell you everything you need to know. Looks like you're a new arrival here, so follow me. You will walk behind me; keep your arms swinging and your mouth shut."

I followed the simple directions and within five minutes found myself in a barber chair. "You can take a bit off the top, please, but leave the sides alone," I directed.

Less than one minute later, my hair lay on the floor. All of it. I was bald—or nearly bald. Reaching up, I found a quarter-inch stubble was all that remained of my once-thick hair. Everything else, including my sideburns, was put to rest on the linoleum floor.

"How much?" I asked, hoping I would be paid for the indignity of losing my hair.

"Nothing. It's free." The old man held out his hand. He was on salary and could not accept any pay for abusing young men's heads.

"You may tip the barber, if you like. In fact, I'd suggest you tip the man whether you like or not," my new dictator commanded. For the price of a quart of oil, I was bald.

"Follow me." He turned and left the room.

One hour later I sat alone in a room with thirty-two beds. "Your name's Teather. That'll put your bed at the door. Last in the alphabet, you know." The Corporal placed my name on a card above the bed where I was to spend nights for the next six months. "Just make your bed any sloppy old way you want. You're the first one of your troop to arrive. In two days, when the other thirty-one members of your troop have arrived, we'll show you all how to make your beds."

HONOUR ROLL

One of the first items to greet a new recruit at Depot is the honour roll. Situated beside the parade square, it lists the names of all our fallen comrades who have, in the line of duty, given the ultimate sacrifice—their lives.

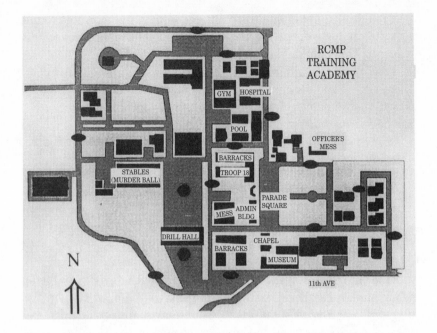

"Breakfast is at 0700 hours, lunch is at 1200 hours, and supper is at 1800 hours. Precisely. Follow your nose to the mess hall. I will be here at 0715 hours tomorrow morning to give you your day's assignment. Until you have permission or you are on assignment or eating, you will not leave this building or this base. Is that clear?"

"Uh, yes."

"Good. Eat breakfast quickly. I will see you in the morning."

"Yes, sir." I had made my first mistake.

"Don't call me sir!" He took three steps toward me and shouted. I winced as his spittle dotted my face.

"Don't you ever call me sir!" he spit-shouted. "My name is Corporal Withers. You will call me Corporal Withers or Corporal. Is that clear?"

"Yes, Corporal Withers."

"Good. See you in the morning."

He turned to leave the empty barracks, paused, then turned. He did not look at me. He spoke the words softly but clearly, and I heard him say, "Welcome to Depot, young feller. I hope you make it." Later that night I fell into a nightmare-infested sleep. Flat roads, potato chips eaten in a westbound car, clattering cans of oil, and a screaming-mad corporal blended together in a senseless nonstop psychotic dream.

The future had arrived. I was growing up. I was scared.

> "They say hard work never hurt anyone, but I figure why take the chance."
>
> Ronald Reagan

CHAPTER THREE
Fatigues—Football Fields and Graves

Thursday, September 14: I had set my alarm clock for 0645 hours. Fifteen minutes to dress, shave, and walk across the street for breakfast.

Fate had other plans.

At 0600 hours my eyes cracked open to the sound of a phonograph needle tracking its way over a scratched record. Seven seconds later reveille blasted its notes over the two speakers mounted at each end of the thirty-two-man dormitory.

The building began to shake. Voices travelled down the walls into my empty bedroom. Profanity. Shouting. Heavy boots pounding on the ceiling above. More shouting. More profanity.

Fifteen minutes later the stairway exploded into a rush of two hundred recruits panic-driven in their mad rush for the parade square. I watched, unbelieving, as they formed into neat formations while one selected member of each group screamed instructions.

"Troop, prove." A massive shuffle of feet and all recruits were in perfect formation.

"Troop, aaatenshuuun!" In an instant, all were standing at attention.

"Right marker!" A voice came from the corner of the parade square. It was a senior police officer who walked stiffly, carried a clipboard, and spoke like thunder. "Corporal."

The segregated recruit jerked to attention. "Troop 17 ready for inspection."

I watched in awe as the ritual continued. The rigid bodies standing in the cool prairie air, the barking out of orders, the handing out of brooms.

The handing out of brooms?

Then, all at once, my brain crashed into itself as I realized where I was. These weren't police recruits. They weren't wearing guns, nor did they sport the latest in blue and gold uniform trousers—the working uniform of the RCMP. They wore uniform hats, but their clothing was not what I had expected.

Khaki. They wore short khaki jackets, khaki pants, and khaki shirts. They were prisoners!

This wasn't a police academy, it was a penitentiary for wayward police officers. I hadn't arrived at the RCMP training academy. I had arrived at the house for naughty cops.

I watched as the broom cart was pushed along in front of the columns of prisoners. The first two columns were handed brooms. Sixty-four brooms were held like rifles as the men obediently marched to the head of the parade square.

The remaining troops were awarded an assortment of tools, items, and devices. One troop was allotted rags. Individual rags. One for each member of the troop. Each rag was accompanied by a small silver tin. A week later, I would learn that this tin contained brass polish, and each morning thirty-two men—one full troop—would be assigned the task of polishing all the door knobs in the training academy.

Another troop received an assortment of small white brushes as their morning gift, and they quickly marched to a large grey-stone building bordering the parade square. This building would have the cleanest sidewalks, steps, and toilets of any building on the base.

The remaining troops were handed string mops, buckets, and rakes. Each implement would be accompanied by orders barked out by a gigantic mouth atop a Scarlet Tunic.

My head reeled and my knees buckled. "My God," I said out loud. "These are prisoners!" My stomach tightened. "I'm in prison."

In one move I stood up and ran for the bathroom. Crashing through the double doors, I searched out the first available receptacle.

But it was too late. In one convulsive jerk my stomach splattered its contents on the floor, the walls, and the sinks that were lined up, single file, military-prison style.

My training had begun. I checked my watch as I finished mopping the floor. It was 7:15 a.m. and I had missed breakfast.

"Teather you dozy little man. Where are you?" Corporal Withers' voice called out.

"Here, sir—uh—Corporal." I walked through the bathroom doors.

"Good. Two of your troopmates are at the train station and we're on our way to pick them up.

"I see by the mess you're cleaning up, you've already had

FATIGUES

(Troop 18, September 1967)
Looking more like prisoners than
police officers, the early arrivals
soon learned the meaning of
hard work.

breakfast." He smiled an evil smile. "Come with me now."

Ten minutes later I shook the hands of the two new arrivals. I felt comfort in their confusion, and already our common ground was forming the base of a friendship that would last a lifetime.

They were to become my troopmates. Fellow prisoners.

Within the hour they were provided with their bedding and relieved of their hair. Name cards were placed over their beds, and we were all marched to the Quarter Master's stores to be issued our uniforms.

Khaki jackets, pants, and shirts were loaded into our outstretched arms. Atop each pile was placed a pair of black ankle boots and a uniform hat.

"When do we get our scarlet tunics?" the fatter of the two new arrivals asked.

"When you bloody well earn them. In the meantime you will wear these fatigues and you will keep your mouths closed."

Corporal Withers led us back to the dormitory, ordered us to dress in our new clothes, then marched us directly to the Corps Sergeant Major's office.

"Sir, may I present to you Constables Lumchuck, Didarski, and Teather?" Corporal Withers stood at attention as he spoke.

"Thank you, Corporal. You are excused."

"Welcome to Depot Division, lads." Corps Sergeant Major Bilby launched a nonstop speech that allowed no pause for thinking, breathing, or interruption. "Later today and tomorrow will see the arrival of the remainder of your troop and your training will begin the following day in the meantime we will keep your idle hands from falling prey to the Devil and this duty will be called fatigues when you leave this office you will exit through the north doors and proceed to the far end of the parade square you will then go to the rear of the first building and just inside the door you will locate a table on this table will be a detailed set of plans you will take the plans, proceed to the shed across the walkway, load lime into the chalker and proceed to the sports field where you will lime the field according to the plans is this clear fine you are dismissed."

We stood, transfixed, attempting to decipher the run-on instructions and not realizing we were free to leave the office.

"Did I not make myself clear?" His eyes widened. "You have your instructions. You can carry them out." Silence. "Now!"

We spun 180 degrees, slapped our feet to the floor, and left quickly. Five minutes later we had retrieved the plans and loaded the chalker. We stood at the corner of the playing field, scratching our heads.

"Where do we start?" I asked.

"How about introductions?" Didarski suggested. "I'm Phil Didarski. Just blew in from Halifax. Don't really know what I'm doing here ... " His eyes looked down to the grass. "I left my girlfriend back home and here I am." Then he looked up and smiled. "As soon as my two years are up we're gonna get married. Shit, a two-day train ride and I miss my gal already."

"Nice to meet you, Phil. I'm Larry Lumchuck. My home is ... was in Edmonton. My dad said I should join the RCMP and lose thirty pounds." His hands circled his belly. "Truth is, I got no girlfriend, and my mom's so sick she probably won't be around for graduation." Larry looked down as his eyes filled with tears. "Cancer." He forced the word out, looked up, and continued. "My dad said he wanted me to be a man. I guess he figured that the RCMP would do the job he couldn't. How about you?" Larry turned to me.

"See that red and white '58 Dodge?" I asked. "That was a 'get-out-of-town' gift from my dad. I'm like you, Larry. Got no girlfriend and don't really know what I'm doing here and in my case it was my brother who told me to leave my home in Hamilton, grow up, and be a man. Anybody here know what a man is?" There was no answer. "Well, we had better get chalking this field before that Corporal Withers wanders by."

"I got the plans." Larry laid them out on the grass. Looking around, he retrieved four fist-sized stones to anchor down the corners against the prairie wind. "You guys just follow my directions, and we'll draw the finest football field this place has ever seen."

For the next hour, Phil and I followed a series of rights, lefts, curves, and squares. When it was finished all three of us looked like chalk ghosts as we proudly surveyed our creation.

"Steady up. Here he comes," Phil whispered.

Corporal Withers approached and studied the three white labourers as he inspected the field. His eyes looked carefully at the lines we had drawn. "Nice job."

We smiled.

"Curly, Larry, and Moe. Only the Three Stooges could have done such a job. Where did they find you three dithering nits? You on drugs or rejects from the Brain Transplants 'R' Us factory?"

"Corporal?" Larry asked.

"You cretins. You brainless idiots. You lumps of thick white gutter slime!" His voice grew loud. "Nice job, dimwits. You have just limed the football field into a basketball court."

We had taken the wrong plans, and while Lumchuck called out the instructions, we had failed to realize that a football field did not have a centre court. In our attempt to be obedient, we had merely followed directions. Lumchuck's directions.

"Who in tarnation is responsible for this?"

We looked at each other but no one answered. Then, candidly, Phil called out, "All of us, Corporal. We all did it."

"Then you shall be punished together." Withers gave us a brief set of directions, then spoke softly. "Already I'm proud of you. You took the responsibility together and you will take the punishment together. By God, you have potential. Not one brain to share amongst the three of you, but you have potential."

For the next six hours we swung corn brooms, trying to sweep away our basketball court. The chalk dust caked inside our noses and made us cough in the hot, dry air.

But we had potential. A friendship had begun. It was born out of punishment and fear, but it was one that would last a lifetime.

We were not allowed lunch that day. We swept the field under the clear September sky, and when our punishment was completed, we swept each other.

Late in the afternoon Corporal Withers returned, thanked us for a job-not-well-done, and quietly told us to follow him. Three minutes later we stood by the RCMP cemetery. Granite headstones stood at attention. Like our beds in the dormitory, each one had been placed exactly in line with the other. Withers stood quietly for a few moments before he spoke.

"There," he pointed, "you will find three shovels and a tape measure. You will dig a hole eight feet long, three feet wide, and six feet deep. The sides of this hole will be exactly vertical, and you will give this hole the respect and the exactness that it deserves. You have two hours to complete your task and during this duty you will not smile, you will not utter a sound, and you will not cease your work until you are finished. You may, however, pause for a moment's reflection."

"A grave?" Phil asked.

"Yes," Withers replied. "A grave. Troop 15 lost one of their members last week. He will be buried here, and you will ensure that this grave will be carved out of the prairie clay with respect."

"What happened?" I asked.

Corporal Withers spoke slowly. "We put too much on one man. He wasn't ready for what the RCMP had to give him. Instead of strength he found weakness. He … " His words trailed off.

"Suicide?" Larry asked.

"Yeah. Such an awful waste and such a poor choice."

"Why?" Phil asked. "At least when faced with the impossible, he took the honourable way out?"

Withers turned back in our direction. "No. No, not at all. Suicide is the worst act possible. It leaves no opportunity for repentance, no chance for forgiveness, and no possibility to succeed. Suicide is the final failure, couched in cowardice. Oh, it is sad, and tomorrow we shall all pray for his soul, but his suicide goes beyond this grave. It will live in the hearts of his family and his girlfriend whom he left behind. Suicide, gentlemen, is not an option. Failure is not an option, and defeat is not an option. In the next six months you will be faced with the harshest conditions possible. We will drive you to the very edge of sanity, then we will drag you back, kicking and screaming all the way. The next six months of your lives will be torturous, but it will be a torture with an honourable exit, not a dreadful end like this."

Corporal Withers turned to walk away, paused, and faced us once more. "I ask you to face life—not death—as your ultimate test." We watched the corporal walk away, not knowing what to say, what to think, or what we would be facing in the next six months.

But we dug. We dug like slaves.

Two hours later we stood by the entrance to the cemetery, our task completed. Quietly, Corporal Withers walked over to the grave site, looked down into the hole, turned in our direction, and spoke. "Well done, lads. See that man over there?" His finger swung to the west. "He is your Drill Corporal. You dug the grave for him. He will inspect the grave after we leave, and if it doesn't meet his standard you will see punishment like no man has ever envisioned. His name is Corporal Wheeler, and for the next six months he will own your soul. Now hit the showers. Report to the mess hall in thirty minutes. The rest of the evening is yours to do with what you want as long as none of you leave your dormitory."

That evening after supper, we met eight more troopmates who had arrived in the late afternoon.

We sat, talked, rubbed our near-bald heads, and spoke of our homes, girlfriends, fears, and goals. At 10:00 p.m. a scratchy phonograph played "Lights Out," and we watched as all the lights on the base blinked out simultaneously. Within minutes, a tough, stocky corporal entered our dormitory. "What you just heard, lads, was the call for lights out. That means that your lights should have been turned out two minutes ago. Do you get my drift?" he shouted.

Without a word, Lumchuck ran to the end of the dorm and turned the lights out. "Well done, fat boy." The unknown Corporal turned and left us with nothing but our fears and Lumchuck's wheezing.

We prepared for a sleepless night filled with fears, fatigues, more psychotic dreams—and wheezing. Only in our last month of training, after Lumchuck had lost nearly forty pounds, would we be spared the nightly torment of his constant wheezing.

Shortly after we had settled into our beds, the swinging doors to our room opened once again. A shadow appeared and a familiar voice spoke softly, "Welcome to Depot, gentlemen. Welcome to the RCMP. Welcome to hell."

It was Corporal Withers.

"Freedom and strength—true freedom and strength—
are only found within the confines of unwavering
discipline."

Corporal Wheeler, Drill Instructor

CHAPTER FOUR
Enter the Dragon—Stiff Spines, Sore Feet, and Harching

Friday, September 15: Three days had passed since my arrival. In that short time our troop had trickled in from across Canada. Harold Burl, fresh in from Toronto, was a nervous, red-faced recruit who shook all our hands twice in case he had forgotten anybody. Don Outman from Estevan, Saskatchewan, passed on his infectious smile as he introduced himself as Prairie Dog, a nickname he promised to explain some day. André Bryant, perhaps even taller than Phil Didarski, introduced himself quietly and confidently when he arrived and stated that he was from "back east." André was to become a legend at the training academy; in the following six months he would quietly lead our troop to victory.

Arriving with André was Brian McPherson. Brian's first acts were to proclaim his pride at being a Newfie, make us all repeat the name of his home town, Come-By-Chance, and challenge everyone in the troop to a fight "either one at a time or all together." Brian liked to fight.

The last member of our troop to arrive would also become a legend at the RCMP training academy. Francois Labeau was from Montreal, Quebec. Although he barely spoke English, in the next six months his courage would speak louder than words in any language. He was a small human being, scarcely making the height and weight requirements of five foot eight inches, 150 pounds. We would later learn that he made acceptance into the RCMP possible by stuffing a half-inch of cardboard into his socks and consuming nearly a gallon of water immediately prior to his weigh-in. Labeau was small, but his heart and courage would also lead us all to victory in the torturous six months that followed.

Reveille had sounded over the dormitory loudspeakers, and while the troops lined up on the parade square, we dressed in our khaki fatigues and paraded our bald heads to the mess hall for an early breakfast.

Sitting together at a long table, thirty-two lost souls drank their powdered milk, ate their pancakes, and engaged in small talk.

CHINK. CHINK. CHINK. A set of silver spurs loosely mounted on a pair of mirror-polished high brown boots announced the arrival of our first enemy of the day. He was the same NCO we had met at the cemetery.

"You will not talk at the table. You will eat and leave. Do I make myself clear?" No one answered. "My God, they gave me a troop of deaf mutes. I said, do I make myself clear?"

"Yes, Corporal," André Bryant softly acknowledged the command.

"Good then. In fifteen minutes I will be in your dorm and you will all be standing by your beds waiting for further instructions. Tardiness will not be accepted, and to make my position perfectly clear the last one of you through the doors will be confined to barracks for two weeks."

Mouths were stuffed, utensils were dropped, and thirty-two recruits raced back to the dormitory. Breakfast took second place to freedom, and when the Corporal saw our entire troop arrive ahead of him he paused, frowned, and warned us not to be so slow next time.

Standing as instructed, we watched in awe as he slowly walked the length of the dormitory, stopping often to survey. He inspected our beds, our clothing, and our person.

"My name is Corporal Wheeler. I am your Drill instructor," were the only words he spoke for the first five minutes.

Corporal Wheeler stood an erect six feet tall and carried a leather riding crop held horizontal under his left armpit. His brown leather boots sported a mirror shine and his uniform was immaculate. A handlebar moustache hid his lips, holding secret his expression of an upturned smile or a downturned scowl. Corporal Wheeler was not human. He belonged in a wax museum, hermetically sealed behind glass, against dust, lint, or wrinkles.

After the inspection he stood at the head of the dorm and spoke in a loud, clear voice.

"In five minutes, members of Troop 17 will arrive. Each member of that troop will instruct you personally. Pay close attention, for any errors you make following their instruction will be yours—not theirs. They will teach you how to make your beds, how to fold your sheets, how to polish your shoes, and how to hang your clothes in your closets. Troop 17 will teach you everything you need to know in order to pass my inspection. Unfortunately, none of you will learn. At 0900 hours I will be waiting in the drill hall for you to begin your first lesson. You will not be late." Corporal Wheeler turned, pushed his way through the swinging doors, and disappeared.

Five minutes later—five minutes precisely—thirty-two senior recruits arrived. As the doors swung open, a voice screamed, "Pass through."

We were later to learn that this phrase would be used each time a dormitory was entered by a foreign troop member. It was a courtesy, shown to respect each troop's private territory.

Troop 17 was our senior troop. Each troop was numbered and its troop designation was encoded with the year. The official designation Troop 17/67–68 revealed that it was the seventeenth troop to be sworn in during 1967 and that their training would continue through the years 1967–68.

Every two or three weeks, eager recruits would arrive to form a new troop of thirty-two recruits. Troop 17 was a mere two weeks senior to our troop, and in only two more weeks, we too would have a junior troop to supervise. Most often, our experience was so alike that it was a matter of the blind leading the blind.

Each member of Troop 17 introduced himself individually to one member of our troop, and the lessons began.

In the brief period that followed we were taught how to shine our shoes to a mirror gloss, how to make our beds, how to disassemble our gun belts, and how to lay the components out on the wool blankets covering our beds. Closet organization was also important, with our civilian clothes being hung at the back, out of sight. Our shoes, our ankle boots, and our high brown riding boots all had their own order and were soon lined up like little leather soldiers in the bottoms of our closets. All our clothing was hung in a small three-foot-wide closet, and any items that were not on the "closet list" were to be stored in the trunk located at the foot of each bed.

After making our beds, we hand-ironed the sheets, being careful not to scorch them. In the RCMP only flat sheets were allowed. Wrinkles had been outlawed. After careful ironing, the sheets were drawn tight enough that a penny would bounce a minimum of two inches after being dropped on them. Each morning we ironed our pillowcases and sheets and dusted everything in the dormitory. Everything.

At the end of our first lesson, members of Troop 17 revealed to us the secret of the alignment test. Kneeling at the foot of one bed, we were shown how to sight down the dormitory to ensure all beds were aligned precisely with each other. "There's no room for individuality in this man's camp," one recruit cautioned. "Your beds and your closets will appear so alike that without the name tag over your bed, no one will be able to tell who owns which pit."

"Pit?" Phil asked.

"Pit," came the answer. "Your living space—your bed and the four feet bordering it—is referred to as your pit. You will be held responsible for every item, every piece of kit and clothing, and every speck of dust in your pit." We stood in silence. "Any questions, men?"

No answer.

"We have five minutes to collect ourselves on the parade square. We see by the daily roster that your first class will be Drill. Corporal Wheeler will be your Drill instructor. We call him the Dragon 'cause he breathes fire, but don't worry, he'll put it out when he spits on you." The senior troop laughed. "Good luck."

Just as quickly as they had arrived, they were gone.

"Holy shit!" Brian yelled. "Lard Thunderin' Cheeses we're late for Drill."

Four minutes later we crowded through the doors to the drill hall. Corporal Wheeler had beaten us this time, and he stood in the centre of the hall, noisily slapping the palm of his gloved left hand with his leather riding crop.

We were late!

Corporal Wheeler stood tall and proud like a porcelain statue. His high brown boots shone like mirrors. His riding pants were pressed smooth. The scarlet tunic that he wore was also flawless and, like his pants, used the RCMP's authority to actually repel lint and any other speck that might visit imperfection on an otherwise flawless image.

"Cod damn," Francois Labeau whispered, "you see dat man. I tink dey painted his clothes on him."

In awe, we stood still, hunkered together for safety, just inside the foyer.

A rumble, a sort of low-frequency reverberation, could be heard echoing off the walls as it slowly took the form of Corporal Wheeler's commanding voice.

"I said you're late!" When Wheeler spoke, his words were first generated as a slow rumble deep within the far reaches of his bowels. Travelling up through his stomach, then his chest, they exploded when they reached his throat.

"Bloody hell, can anybody hear me? I said you're late!" The explosion hit us again. Like mice in a pet store cage, we cowered. None of us knew our future. We were cornered, with no place to escape.

Slowly, Corporal Wheeler walked over to each of us, grabbed us one by one by the ear, and led us to the centre of the drill hall. Within a few hellish, sore-eared minutes we were lined up, shoulder-to-shoulder, in two columns. Harold Burl would lead the troop, and I would take my six-month position at the rear.

"Alphabetically. That is how you will appear from this moment forth," the Corporal commanded.

Then he became the porcelain Mountie. His eyes stared into our souls as his body remained immobile. Taking two steps backwards he raised his left leg until his thigh was horizontal to the floor, then he slammed his leg down in one thunderous crack that made our entire troop stiffen with anticipation.

Then there was the silence. Again, he did not move. His chest showed no signs of breathing, his eyes remain fixed—staring straight ahead—and his body all at once became as rigid and solid as any statue ever cast, carved, or sculpted.

Then he spoke the words I would never forget: "Today I see before me a troop of individuals. You will soon become an individual troop."

Once again raising his left leg and slamming it into the wood floor of the drill hall, he walked forward to begin his inspection. The scrutiny began at the beginning of the alphabet and worked its way slowly to the end of the troop.

"Burl?" he questioned the first recruit.

"Yes, Corporal."

"You need to learn how to shave. You got stubble on that ugly face of yours. What did you shave with, a rock?"

"Yes, Corporal."

Pulling a disposable safety razor from his pocket, Corporal Wheeler marched Harold Burl over to one of the six full-length mirrors that hung on the drill hall wall and removed the stubble Harold had missed earlier in the morning. We watched out of the corners of our eyes as tiny little blood spots formed on Harold's face and a sound characteristic of Velcro being separated reached our ears. We winced. Burl was taken by the ear and led back to his position at the head of the troop. Looking down at the blood and the skin encrusting the razor, Corporal Wheeler spoke.

"Some day I'm gonna get me a new razor. Some day. But a good razor like this should last more than two years, shouldn't it?" His gaze penetrated beyond Harold's eyes and stabbed into his brain.

"Yes, Corporal. Much more than two years."

"I'm going to like you, lad," Wheeler countered.

"Bryant!" he shouted.

"Yes, Corporal." André's answer came smooth and confident, yet humble. His lack of fear briefly attracted our Drill instructor's gaze as he spoke to the recruit.

"Just checking to see if you're conscious." For some unknown reason, Corporal Wheeler chose not to torment André. Throughout the next six months, André Bryant was to become somewhat of an enigma ... a riddle wrapped in a puzzle. Only a select few of us would learn more of this man—his abilities and his past—and we would never know whether his unconquerable spirit commanded a degree of respect from our instructors ... or fear.

Moving down the line, Corporal Wheeler continued his verbal assault, approaching each member of our troop and reading his name from the tag worn on the right side of the uniform shirt.

"Didarski."

"Yes, Corporal?"

"Where you from?"

"Halifax, Corporal."

"Go home. I don't like Easterners."

"Kriz ... Krizink ... Krisinisnik ..." Wheeler fumbled over Ken Krzyszyk's name tag.

"Corporal," Krzyszyk replied.

"Is that your name or are you wearing an eye chart?"

"It's my name, Corporal."

"Change it," he ordered.

"Yes, Corporal."

"Labeau."

"Yes, Caporal," Francois replied in the best English he could muster.

"You French?" Corporal Wheeler asked the obvious.

"Yes, Caporal."

"What do you hope to accomplish here?"

"My fodder says he tinks I might become a man," Francois said.

"My fodder says he tinks I might become a man." Wheeler mimicked Labeau's reply. "My fodder says he tinks I might become a man." He repeated the mimicry. Then, with his face less than an inch from Labeau's, he said softly but firmly, "You write a letter home to your dad and tell him he's right." Labeau blinked. "You tell your fodder dat I'll make a man out of you even if it kills one of us—and Labeau...?" Wheeler stopped in mid-sentence.

"Yes, Caporal?"

"I don't expect to die."

"Me neider, Caporal ... but ..."

"But what?"

"Dis marching, Caporal—it's killing my feet."

"Tape an aspirin on them when you go to bed. That'll take care of your pain. And as for the rest of you, if you've got an ouchie, I don't want to hear about it." Then he added, "Just tape an aspirin on it."

Wheeler continued his inspection. "Lumchuck."

"Yes, Corporal."

"What kind of name is that?"

"Polish, Corporal."

"I don't like Polacks." Wheeler thrust his forefinger knuckle deep into Larry's stomach. "I especially don't like fat Polacks. What do you weigh?"

"Two hundred and twenty pounds, Corporal," Lumchuck replied.

"You've got three months to lose forty pounds or I back-troop you. You got that clear in your fat Polack head?"

"Yes, Corporal." We had heard of back-trooping. At any time during the training, failure to meet minimum standards would result in the recruit being moved to a more junior troop. It was the ultimate humiliation and usually preceded discharge. Once a recruit had been back-trooped, every instructor on base would place him under a virtual magnifying glass, and like an ant caught under a focussed beam of sunlight, he would either learn to outsmart his hunters or explode. The grave we had dug three days earlier was testament to the magnitude of the pressure that could be brought to bear.

Corporal Wheeler continued. "McPherson."

"Corporal."

"Where you from, lad?"

"Come-By-Chance, Corporal."

"Where?"

"Come-by-Chance. She's a small fishin' village in Newfoundland."

"Thought I smelled something." Wheeler continued his assault. "Outman."

"Yes, Corporal."

FORWARD HARCH!

In response to one single command, 32 recruits would move together as an individual troop.

"Where you from?"

"Estevan, Corporal."

"You a Saskatchewan Stubble-Jumper?"

"Yes, Corporal."

"Only good thing that came out of Saskatchewan was an empty bus."

My stomach rumbled and cramped as our Drill Corporal finally approached me.

"Teather."

"Yes, Corporal," I replied.

"Where you from?"

"Hamilton, Ontario."

"I know where Hamilton is, you dozy little man. The only thing that comes from Hamilton is braggarts, bullshitters, and bastards. Which one are you?"

"Don't know, Corporal."

"Bullshitter!" He screamed the words into my face, ejecting tiny particles of saliva along with his shrieks. I could feel the tiny drops landing on my forehead, my cheeks, and my lips. I had never been that intimate with another man before—and I would never be that intimate with another man again.

"Bullshitter!" he screamed again. "What I see before me is one hundred and sixty pounds of crap, crammed into a one-hundred-pound sack. You're so full of bullshit your eyes are brown."

"Yes, Corporal."

"Haven't we met before, Constable Bullshitter?"

"Yes, Corporal. Three days ago I dug a grave for you."

"Maybe I can do the same for you some day," he replied, then walked to the front of the troop.

"You are Troop 18. You are not a troop of thirty-two individuals, you are an individual troop. You are not British Columbians, Albertans, you aren't even Newfies! There is more that holds you together than could ever tear you apart. You are members of the Royal Canadian Mounted Police. Beyond that and more important you are Canadians! Do you understand? You are Canadians." He continued, barely stopping to take a breath. "For the next six months you will fight, you will learn, you will eat, and you will sleep together." He paused, sucked air into his lungs, then continued. "For the next six months you will become one synchronized mass of flesh, and under my command you will learn to operate as a unit. You will ask no questions of me until the day before you graduate. Graduation at Depot Division is called Passing Out, and believe me when I say you will experience passing out many times before I am through with you. No, there will be no questions from you that I will answer, at least for now. You do not have enough intelligence to ask any meaningful questions, and you do not have the discipline to carry out the answers." He took another breath, then shouted, "Is that clear?"

"Yes, Corporal!" A cacophony of voices responded. Corporal Wheeler looked down and shook his head, then once more addressed our troop.

"My goal is to teach you discipline. Your goal is to become disciplined. Freedom and strength—true freedom and strength—are only found within the confines of unwavering discipline. Through discipline, you will all come to learn the true meaning of freedom and strength. Our goal is to make you Mounties. Your objective is to meet our goal. We here at Depot Division are the Mountie makers. We will fulfill our duty and you will fulfill yours." Then he added, "But the lesson will be painful. Do you all understand?"

"Yes, Corporal." Our voices clattered and mixed as we tried to synchronize our reply.

Wheeler shook his head with disgust, then added, "For the next six months whatever hurts, ladies, tape an aspirin on it." Then his voice boomed out. "Welcome to hell!"

For five minutes, thirty-two recruits practised shrieking "Yes, Corporal!" until only one voice could be heard. The confident voice of a thirty-two-man troop.

Our training had begun.

For the next two hours we were taught how to stand, breathe, and march. Thirty-two prisoners marched in straight lines, diagonal lines, and in circles in the drill hall until only one set of footsteps could be heard. When a recruit fell out of step, the troop was halted. When a recruit turned the wrong way, he was punished, and when a recruit veered off course, his personal degradation became a subject of fear and laughter for the other thirty-one prisoners.

"Troop halt!" Corporal Wheeler called as he walked over to Phil Didarski. "Didarski, you keep pulling to the left, whatsamatter with you?"

"Don't know, Corporal."

"You tryin' to veer out the door or somethin'? You wanna escape to that pretty little girlfriend you left in Halifax?" Corporal Wheeler had studied our personal files, and he knew us better than we would ever know him.

"No, Corporal."

"Good, 'cause she's likely forgotten you already."

"No, Corporal." Wheeler had touched a sensitive spot. Collectively, we held our breath as Phil contradicted our Drill Corporal. Moving my head a fraction of an inch, I could see tears in Phil's eyes.

The Corporal ignored his comment and saw Phil's weakness. Like a predator, he went in for the kill. "I wouldn't worry about that cheap piece of lipstick, she's probably forgotten you anyway. I'd bet she's out with your best friend right now."

"No, Corporal." Phil's eyes were filled with tears and his voice choked.

"Don't you 'No-Corporal' me, you towering piece of crud. Before the six months is over you'll be telling me she's gone!" Wheeler was nose-to-nose with Didarski and Phil was about to lose control. "Don't even think about hitting me, lad, I'll take you to the floor so quick you'll mess your pants."

Then, as the two men stood one inch apart, Corporal Wheeler seized Phil by his emotional handles and stopped a fight before it could begin.

"Stop!" Wheeler screamed. Phil jerked to attention.

"Now I see what the problem is."

"Problem, Corporal?"

"Yeah. Your veering off to the left all the time. It's your ear."

"My ear?"

"Yeah." Corporal Wheeler reached out and tapped Phil's left ear with his leather riding crop. "Your left ear. It's bigger than your right ear. Sticks out more, too. I'll bet with you being so damned tall it's catching the jet stream and pulling you left all the time." A suppressed giggle ran through the troop. It was a muffled laughter that barely escaped from our throats. We were partly amused by Wheeler's humour but mostly amazed and grateful at how his personal attack against Phil's emotions had ceased.

"Yeah, I'll bet that's it. Your ear's pulling you to the left. Don't worry, lad, we'll have the post doctor trim a half-inch off it so you can walk straight."

Phil smiled, blinked, and cleared the tears from his eyes.

"And just one thing, young lad ..." Corporal Wheeler spoke in a hushed voice for the first time. "Don't you ever get soft on me—you hear?"

"Yes, Corporal."

"Good."

"Aaatenshuun!" Wheeler commanded. Instantly the troop snapped to attention. One loud clap could be heard as thirty-two black ankle boots slammed down hard on the drill hall floor. Toes crunched and teeth chattered. The edges of Corporal Wheeler's mouth turned upward ever so slightly.

"That's a beginning," he said, then added, "But it's only a beginning."

Wheeler studied the troop for a moment before he gave his last command of the day. "Fooorwaaard harch." As one, thirty-two recruits stepped ahead and began walking forward—on a six-month journey.

We had commenced to learn how to harch.

Our training had begun.

CHAPTER FIVE
Murder Ball—Sawdust, Horse Urine, and Death

Saturday, October 14: 0600 hours. Our second month of basic training. Reveille played on an antique record player, and its rude tune scratched its way into our dreams. Wiping my eyes, I swung my legs out of bed, turned on my lamp, and looked at the loudspeaker. It sported countless scars from boots and other items that had been thrown at it in anger, but it failed to resign its unholy duty. Together, thirty-two recruits sat up in their beds as reveille wound its unwelcome melody throughout the dorm. Together we untaped the aspirins that had decorated our feet, our shoulders, and our aching spines.

"Bloody hell," a voice complained. "It's bloody Saturday. What the hell do they want?"

The double doors burst open. It was Corporal Wheeler.

"Okay, men, rise and shine. Morning parade is at 0630 hours, fatigues will continue until 0730 hours, breakfast will be served at 0800 hours, and you will be in the stable at 0900 hours."

"Stable?" an anonymous voice chirped.

"You heard me—the riding stable at 0900 hours. Order of dress will be fatigues."

As quickly as he had arrived, he was gone.

Ten minutes later we had taken our place on the parade square. As the junior troop on base, we were given the unholiest of fatigue duties for completion prior to breakfast. Toilets!

We were split into sixteen teams of two. Each team would carry their toilet swishers, cans of foul-smelling white powder, and bottles of bleach. Touring the washrooms throughout the administration building, we cleaned each porcelain throne until it sparkled.

"Boy dese NCO's sure shit a lot, don't dey," Francois commented in his French accent as he scrubbed the bowl.

"Yeah, I guess that happens to you when you get promoted," I suggested.

"Cod damn, I tink dat dere are more crappers here dan dere are Caporals. Do you tink dey need all dese twalets?"

"We clean dem, and dey mess dem," I replied. Francois had become a good friend, and mimicking his French accent was accepted as a personal and allowable form of humour. Together we scrubbed, wiped, and polished our way to breakfast.

Ninety minutes later we took our place in the food line.

"Hey Francois, did you wash dem hands after latrine duties?" Didarski called out as we lined up for chow.

"Oui," Francois called back. "I washed dem in de twalet." A laugh ran down the line but stifled itself as Corporal Withers walked in.

"Eat fast lads, you got orgy sports in one-half hour."

Five minutes later we sat at a long table. We had learned that talking was not allowed in the mess hall, but whispering, when not detected, was often practised.

"Orgy sports?" Ken Krzyszyk muttered. "What the heck are orgy sports?" There was no reply. We had thirty minutes to eat our breakfast, make our beds, clean our pits, and report to the old abandoned riding stables. In short, that meant we had five minutes to gag down a meal of greasy bacon and undercooked pancakes.

Not much was said during mealtime. The food was rarely palatable and usually undercooked—unless it was meat; then the fat content at least made it easier to swallow. With his pancakes, each recruit was served two strips of hardly cooked side bacon. We never understood why bacon was served with pancakes—perhaps it was an RCMP tradition—but we ate it anyway.

"Hey, dis is okay. When you put de bacon on top, de grease makes dem slick." Francois rubbed his two strips of bacon on his pancakes and lubricated them before cutting off chunks with his fork and forcing them down. Francois Labeau relished his breakfast like a condemned man.

And ... he was.

Fifteen minutes later thirty-two men made their beds, mopped the cold linoleum floor, and dusted. We had been warned that Depot dust had been responsible for more punishment than any other item. Dusting meant cleaning every surface, every crack, and every item in the dorm. Window sills, desk tops, and even our gun belts, which were laid out at the foot of our beds, would be free of dust. Dust was evil, and it was to be a constant six-month duel between our troop and the Dust Monster, the unholy ghost that inhabited our dorm.

Thirty minutes of fighting bedsheet creases, dust, and a dreadful lump of greasy pancakes had passed, and we deserted our quarters for the cool October morning air.

"Troop 18, aaatenshuun!" Phil Didarski shouted. He had been volunteered as our Right Marker. It was a frightful duty. As Right Marker, he would shout us to attention and other nonergonomic positions that cramped every muscle in the body. As Right Marker he would be responsible for any lint on our uniforms, any un-shone shoes, and any infraction of the dress and deportment code. Phil would spend many weekends confined to barracks because of another person's lint.

"Troop 18, riiight turn!" Together, we turned right. "Troop 18, forward harch!" As an individual troop we harched away from the front of "B" block, our dormitory building, and into a day none of us would ever forget.

"Troop halt!" Didarski commanded as thirty-two heels slammed down on the concrete paving-stone entrance to the riding stable. Corporal Withers stood waiting.

Silence.

More silence.

It was painful.

We waited.

"Good morning, lads. Corporal Wheeler and Troop 17 request your presence inside for a one-hour game. I am to brief you." He paused for a moment, then continued. "Organized sports, or orgy sports as it has often been called, will pit you against a senior troop. It is a game of brutal strength and cunning wit. Only the strong and intelligent will survive. Sadly, I look at you this morning, healthy and fresh. In one hour I will meet several of you at the post hospital. The doctor is standing by with his suture kit and ..." He paused again, smiled, and said clearly, "Blood will wash out if you use cold water and do your laundry this afternoon. Good luck. Your future awaits."

Then, taking a long deep breath, he shouted, "Forward harch!" as thirty-two men walked, uninjured, into the riding stable. Withers followed, keeping his distance. He had taken a liking to our troop, although none of us knew it then—but it was a fondness that would continue to develop for six months. He was not assigned to our troop as counsellor. His affection for our troop was a mysterious one, almost as enigmatic as André's past. Keeping his distance, Withers entered the stable and stood, near-invisible, in a dark corner as he watched our first game of Murder Ball.

"Troop 18, you will line up at the north end!" Corporal Wheeler shouted.

"Left wheel," Didarski commanded as we turned left and marched through the dirt and sawdust. "Troop halt." We stopped at the wall. "About turn." As a single unit, we spun 180 degrees and slammed our ankle boots into the dirt. A cloud of dust rose and found its way into our nostrils.

"I tink I smell a horse," Francois whispered. We stifled a laugh as one hundred years of horse urine stuck to the inside of our noses.

"Welcome to Murder Ball, lads." Corporal Wheeler stood to the side as we faced our senior troop at the far end of the riding stable. "For the benefit of Troop 18, I will explain the rules." Wheeler turned in our direction and continued his speech. "This riding stable is equipped with two hockey goal nets. In the centre of the stable is a football. I know that because I placed it there myself. There is only one rule. You must place that football in your opponents' net. There will be no fouls recorded, no time out for injury, no out-of-bounds, and no illegal manoeuvres. The play will begin when I say and end after a goal has been scored. If you are injured and I approve your wounds, you may proceed directly to the post hospital. If I do not approve your wounds, you will continue playing. If you cannot walk, one—I repeat one—troopmate may assist you. However, once again I remind you that the play will not end until a goal has been scored. Any questions?"

No one answered.

Walking to the centre of the arena, Wheeler turned left, walked to the nearest wall, turned, and faced the ball.

"Now!"

Thirty-two members of Troop 17, our senior troop, charged. In shock we half-marched, half-ran forward. Sixty-four bodies collided. It was a sickening sound. Chests losing air, stomachs losing contents, and our troop—Troop 18—losing the first goal. Picking ourselves up from the dirt, we had learned the first and only rule of play: Win.

"That was pathetic," Wheeler shouted as we retreated to the wall and lined up once again. "Bloody pathetic. I've never seen such cowardice in my entire life. If that happens again you won't leave the barracks for a month. Do I make myself clear?"

"Yes, Corporal," answered those of us who could breathe.

"Good." He walked to the centre of the stable and placed the football on the dirt.

"Troop 17, you will not receive credit for that goal. You just battered a troop of sissies. You don't deserve a point for pounding a party of little girls."

Troop 17 laughed. We did not.

"Time out," Wheeler announced. Troop 17 continued laughing as he approached our end of the stable. "Trouble with you ladies is that you didn't know the rules. I will remind you little girls in a way that your sweet little brains can understand. See that ball in the centre of the stable?" We nodded. "Well then, bloody well put it into their net!" he screamed. "Can you understand me or are you all wearing skirts!"

"Yes, Corporal."

"Just do it. I will give you one minute to formulate a plan. That's about fifty-nine seconds longer than your opponent will give you on the street."

Collectively we wondered what he meant by his last statement, but we quickly huddled. Phil Didarski was a born leader, and as he was our Right Marker, we accepted his play.

"Teather, you're a little guy, you can't do much, so just run around and scream at the top of your lungs. Lumchuck, you follow Teather like you're trying to catch him. Start yelling that he's gone crazy. That should give us the benefit of distraction. Outman, you run up the ball, fall down, get up, and start screaming 'I got it'—that'll give us another distraction. Labeau, I'll grab the ball, pretending to help Outman, then hand it to you. Stay close to me, will ya?"

"*Oui.*"

"Okay, men, let's shed our skirts. It's showtime."

Together we faced our enemy. Troop 17. This time we would win.

"Now!" Wheeler shouted.

As planned, we ran to the centre of the stable. Screaming as loud as my dust-and-horse-urine-infected lungs would allow, I peeled to the right with Lumchuck following behind.

Outman fell on the ball, rolled over, and passed it to Didarski, who palmed it off to Labeau. A hole opened up in the defence as several members of Troop 17 stopped to watch Lumchuck follow the escaped mental patient. Seizing the moment, Labeau ran faster than a greyhound on steroids. He ran for the goal net. He ran for success. He ran for his life. Each one of our troop had grabbed an opponent by his fatigue jacket. We had tied them up and were holding them as prisoners while Francois ran us to victory.

It was obvious that this tactic had never been employed before. Fights broke out throughout the combat zone. Noses were bloodied and the pounding of bodies hitting the dirt could be heard over the grunts and groans of sixty-four recruits. They could even be heard over the sounds of Lumchuck chasing his mental patient.

Then, time stopped. It stopped dead.

Francois was tackled—hit from behind by Troop 17's biggest member. None of us will ever know what attracted our attention to the tackle. It might have been the sound of air leaving Labeau's lungs, or it might have been the sound of his thin body crushing itself into the dirt, or it might have been the high-pitched snap of a spinal vertebra cracking under the pressure of the tackle, but it was a sound that stopped the fight.

Labeau's attacker rose from the dirt, but his quarry remained limp, motionless, and barely breathing. Like Francois, the ball lay motionless, still, quiet in the dirt.

"Get up, you horizontal piece of dog flesh!" Wheeler screamed at the top of his lungs.

Francois remained motionless. His eyes stared straight ahead and dirt covered his lips.

"I said get up!"

André Bryant's long, powerful legs propelled him over to Labeau's side in three strides. Kneeling down beside his fallen comrade, Bryant put his face down close to the dirt, then looked up.

"Call an ambulance," he said clearly and softly.

"You pick that lump of guts up now!" Wheeler walked toward Bryant.

Bryant's eyes caught Wheeler's as he approached. "You even touch this man and I'll rip your lungs out through your arse and feed them to the dogs." Wheeler stopped dead. "I said call an ambulance. He has a spinal injury ... barely breathing ... for God's sake, somebody call an ambulance."

Half the arena emptied as men raced for the nearest telephone. Seconds later, Wheeler, Lumchuck, André, and I knelt beside our friend. His face was grey, his breaths came in short, laboured puffs, and his body lay motionless in the horse-urine-soaked dirt.

"Francois, can you hear me?" André spoke softly. Labeau's eyes turned toward his friend. "Listen up, buddy. You have a spinal injury ... I'd guess it's your neck. Too soon to tell, but I think you'll be okay. We'll just tape one of those aspirins on it for now. Don't move, buddy. Don't talk. We'll have an ambulance here in a minute or two." André turned his face away from Francois. His eyes were filled with tears as he ever so slightly moved his own head from side to side. Standing up, he spoke softly to our Drill Corporal.

"Corporal, this man is in serious shape. I've seen it before and it's not good. Please don't touch him. He needs medical care real bad if he's to live." Wheeler's eyes opened wide. "It's C3 or C4, I believe. His breathing is suppressed and he's paralyzed from the neck down. You understand?"

Wheeler nodded his head.

"Lumchuck, you go out and organize a welcoming committee for the ambulance. Starting at the entrance gate, make sure there's a man every fifty feet to guide them to the arena." Lumchuck rose to his feet and ran to the door.

For an eternity we knelt beside Francois, encouraging him with promises that he would be okay. Lying promises, but promises just the same.

The sound of a siren could be heard in the distance, and as it grew louder, Bryant's optimism was directed toward our fallen friend.

"Okay, buddy, they're just about here. Probably got a whole bottle of aspirins to tape on your body. We'll have you looking like the polka-dot king in no time at all. You just hang in there, we're gonna get you to the hospital."

Francois could not move, but his eyes looked into André's and we knew he understood.

Five minutes later Francois was braced at the neck and painstakingly loaded onto a stretcher. With the help of his troopmates, he was gently taken to the waiting ambulance. In seconds the rear doors were closed and the ambulance drove slowly away.

"*Bonne chance, mon ami,*" André said softly. "Good luck, my friend."

"Didn't know you spoke French," Wheeler said.

"Lots of things you don't know, Corporal," André replied in a tone that was neither sarcastic nor soothing.

"Game's over for today," Corporal Wheeler called. "Everyone back to barracks. You've got the rest of the day off."

As we left the riding stable we could see Corporal Wheeler standing close to Withers. They spoke for a few seconds, then Withers placed his hand on Wheeler's shoulder as they both bowed their heads.

A few of us headed over to the post hospital—some for stitches, some for aspirins, and some to watch.

The post doctor was a retired prairie doctor whose patients included both humans and livestock. His nickname, Needles, had been earned. When not taping aspirins on bruises, he was kept busy inoculating the new recruits. Ten troops of thirty-two recruits with three injections each made a total of 960 injections every six months. Needles was a fitting nickname. It was claimed (but never substantiated) that he saved the government money by only replacing his syringe and its barbed tip every six months. Rumour was, if you received an injection in June or December he pounded the needle in with a hammer and removed it with a winch. The most painful part of the injection came when he withdrew the needle from deep within your shoulder-muscle tissue, and the barb raised the flesh to form a small mountain on your arm as it tore its way out. Like a robot, Needles would look at the blood streaming down your arm and suggest, "Tape an aspirin on it."

Needles loved his work.

Lumchuck and I moved from cubicle to cubicle as we surveyed our troopmates' injuries. Didarski was developing a black eye—a gift received after loosening an opponent's tooth. Don Outman had acquired a deep cut on the top of his head where he was kicked after diving for the ball, and Ken Krzyszyk was busy taping an aspirin on his sprained shoulder.

"Anyone want a real painkiller?" Needles asked, holding up his five-month-old hypodermic. There were no requests for further medical attention.

An hour later we sat in our dormitory—together—alone.

"Wonder how Francois is doing?" Ken Krzyszyk asked.

"Yeah, he looked real bad," Phil Didarski added.

"Heard the priest was called in. Gave him his last rites. Do you think his parents will arrive in time to watch him die?" Don asked.

"Shit, man, what are we doing here? Our first day we dig a grave, and the second one, we put one of our buddies in it," another voice added.

"Quit!" André raised his voice. "Just quit. Francois isn't dead yet, and with us thinking like that we aren't helping him any. I know it doesn't look good but we can hope, can't we?"

"False hope," Larry Lumchuck suggested.

Silence.

For an hour we sat together. Few words were said, and every time one recruit met the gaze of a fellow troopmate, they would both look away. Francois was hurt and we felt the pain.

Members of Troop 17 visited our dormitory that afternoon. They all carried with them the same pain that we felt. There was no animosity, no riding-stable screaming.

The game was over.

We never ate supper that night, and as the sun lowered itself down below the western horizon our dorm grew dark. It was after dark when we were visited. The doors swung open quietly and a silhouette stood motionless.

"Got any light in here?"

We knew the voice. It was Corporal Withers.

An anonymous voice sprang from the darkness. "With all due respect, Corporal, you're not wanted here. You led us into this mess. You watched. You sanctioned the slaughter, and now you can leave, if you please."

"If that's what you want, gentlemen. If all you are capable of understanding is injury and pain ... then I will leave."

"Wait," André called out. "What do you mean?" Something told me that André already knew the answer but wanted us all to hear the explanation.

"Do you know why we play orgy sports?" Withers asked.

"Makes us tough?"

"Makes us competitive?"

"Pushes us even harder?"

Answers continued bubbling out of the darkness.

"You're all correct."

Silence.

"Know why we play Murder Ball?" Withers repeated the question, calmly.

Silence.

"Well, I'll tell you." Corporal Withers raised his voice ever so slightly. "When you graduate—and that day will come—you will be faced with insurmountable odds. Oh, I'm not just talking about a mean Sergeant, a pile of paperwork, or a mealy-mouth defence attorney. You will all be afforded the opportunity to walk down a dark alley and interrupt a break-in, a theft, or even a rape in progress. That's why we play Murder Ball."

"I don't understand." The voice belonged to Don Outman. "What's an alley rape got to do with Murder Ball?"

"Everything," Withers said. "When you arrest that dirty filthy low-life, he'll fight you. There will be no rules in that alley. You'll both bite, scratch, kick, gouge, tear, and scream, and only one of you will put the ball in your opponent's net. There will be only one winner. One victor. Defeat is not an option."

"No rules?"

"No rules, gentlemen. On the streets, like in the riding arena, there is only one intent, one purpose, one objective. You must win. That's what makes a Mountie. Mounties do not lose. Not ever."

"What about Francois? He's beyond hope now. He's had the last rites, hasn't he? Don't pump us any false hope now."

"Don't start with that shit!" Don Withers raised his voice in anger. "There is no such thing as false hope. Hope is often the only thing that affords us a firm grasp on reality. There is no such thing as false hope. All hope is true."

Then, in the darkness of our dormitory, we came to understand Murder Ball. It was a toughening process. A rite of passage to prepare us to be strong and independent and, above all, to teach us to win against all odds. But Francois did not win in the arena that day. He had lost his first fight.

Withers drew a deep breath, then spoke. "Francois is hurt. He's hurt real bad. They called in a priest to administer the last rites.

THE GAME AIN'T OVER YET

Only by supporting each other and by combining our strengths would we succeed. The recruit on the top could not have climbed to his lofty height without the support of his troop combined with his belief in our strength.

Nearly everyone has given up on him. His mom and dad will be here tomorrow, and if I'm not mistaken, they've given up on him too. We might as well do what everyone else has done. Let's give up on Francois just like everyone else. Yeah, that's it, let's just go out there and dig another grave. Everyone else has. C'mon, I know it's dark, but we can dig in the dark."

"Bullshit!" Didarski called out. "We ain't gonna dig no graves tonight. Not while our friend is still breathing. Screw you, Withers, you ain't gonna get no more graves out of us. Not while our troopmate still breathes and we still care. The game ain't over yet."

"Guess you're right." Corporal Withers stood up to leave, but as he reached the door he paused and turned. "You're right. The game ain't over yet. Goodnight, gentlemen. Maybe we'll make Mounties out of you yet."

The door closed behind him, but the message he had come to deliver remained. The game wasn't over—yet.

A few minutes later a scratchy record played "Lights Out" but it was not necessary. We had already gone to bed. Our lights had already been turned out.

And in the darkness, someone cried.

> "Faithless is he that says farewell when the road darkens."
>
> J.J.R. Tolkein

CHAPTER SIX
Church Parade, Hospital Visits and Horsemeat

Sunday, October 15: Reveille played once more over the dormitory speakers as thirty-one recruits rubbed their eyes open and swung their feet onto the cold linoleum floor.

André Bryant was sitting on the edge of his bed. In the darkness, he had already showered and dressed. Looking across the dorm, I could see him smile.

"What's up, André?" I asked.

"Francois," he replied. Silence fell upon the dorm. "I've been calling the hospital all night."

More silence.

"Well, the priest did that last rites thing on him, and his mom and dad arrived just after midnight."

Still the dorm remained silent.

"Guess what?"

No one replied. No one moved.

"This morning he wiggled his toes."

The dormitory exploded into a collective roar that could be heard on the parade square. Socks were thrown, bare feet pounded on the cold floor, and amidst the cacophony of hurrahs, tears were shed. Then, as the cries, laughter, and cheering subsided, André spoke quietly.

"Seems his neck wasn't broken after all. One vertebra was fractured, and the doctor said something about spinal cord shock. He's pretty optimistic about recovery. Might not be full—Francois has probably played his last game of Murder Ball, but so far ... well, you were right, Phil." He turned to Didarski. "You and Withers were right. The game ain't over yet."

With smiles on our faces, we dressed and took our places on the parade square. Corporal Withers was assigned to Sunday Fatigue Parade, and as he supervised the dispersion of rags, rakes, and toilet brushes he could plainly see the collective smile on our troop. Approaching Phil Didarski, he stopped, then spoke. "You gentlemen know something I don't?"

"Yes, Corporal!" the entire troop replied in unison. Phil relayed the good news that André had brought us, and a smile grew on Withers' face until his teeth showed. Walking over to André Bryant, he once again spoke in a voice we could all hear.

"You look pretty bright-tailed and bushy-eyed for a man who's been up all night."

"Yes, Corporal."

"How do you do it?"

"It's a skill I learned a long time ago."

"Good, you're on Night Guard duty tonight. You and Teather. Oh, by the way ..." He paused.

"Yes, Corporal?"

"Thanks. Thanks a lot."

"Yes, Corporal. But you were right."

"About what?"

"The game ain't over yet."

Corporal Withers' smile widened even more, and as he turned his back and walked away we heard him say, "You gentlemen just might make it. Just might."

One hour later the toilets had been cleaned and Troop 18 sat at the long breakfast table. Smearing the bacon grease on our pancakes, we practised swallowing large mouthfuls of doughy paste quickly. In twenty minutes we were scheduled, with the entire base, for Church Parade.

The first day we arrived, we had learned about Church Parade from a senior troop. The front rows were reserved for those who had been issued their scarlet tunics. If they were of the Protestant faith they could attend the Force chapel on base. Other recruits formed lines according to their own faith. In civilian clothes the recruits formed small groups of Mormons, Jehovah's Witnesses, Christian Scientists, and "Other." All religious groups were obliged to board a bus for delivery to their church of choice.

All groups except the Other. Men in the Other group were allowed to return to the dormitory and worship in their own fashion. This was usually accomplished by lying on their beds and closing their eyes in a trance-like meditation. To the uneducated, this had the appearance of sleeping.

Within a few weeks, the number of men joining the Other religion grew steadily until very few Non-Others remained.

On this day, our entire troop joined the Other religion. Returning to our dormitory, we entered our sleep-like prayer state, and as we closed our eyes, each one of us said a small thanks for Francois' toe-wiggling progress.

We had learned to dress quickly, eat quickly, and even sleep quickly. Two hours later, Troop 13 came back to life.

"Where you goin'?" Outman asked.

"We have a friend to see, don't we?" André replied.

Sunday after worship was the only spare time granted to recruits. We were free, in a fashion, to head to town, read, or sit in the dorm and listen to music. Most recruits headed to town, if only to experience the freedom.

No recruit was allowed to leave the base without wearing a dress shirt, tie, and suit. If seen by an instructor on the streets of Regina without a tie, any recruit would certainly lose his freedom and be "confined to barracks—C.B.'d" for a minimum of two weeks.

One hour later, thirty-one suits walked the autumn streets of Regina. Our first destination was Regina General Hospital. We lined up in the hallway and each of us entered Francois' bedroom for a ten-second peek. The nurses, against orders, had allowed us all to visit our comrade. As we filed through the bedroom, we each took our ten-second time ration to say a soft "Hi buddy" and squeeze his foot, hoping for a small toe wiggle in return. We smiled, winked, straightened his covers, and made other small gestures as his eyes tracked our movements.

Tears ran down Francois' cheeks. Tears of thanks for our presence. But he did not speak. A short while later we sat with his parents in the lounge.

"He's too tired to talk," his mother explained. "But he did say a few words last night."

"What did he say?" Don asked.

"He asked if his troop scored the goal."

We smiled and told her that we had won our first game of Murder Ball and to tell Francois that he had been voted our Most Valuable Player. When he was tackled, we explained, he had been so close to the net that the ball had popped from his hands and scored a goal. We lied about the goal. Mr. and Mrs. Labeau needed something to cling to, and even if it was a small lie, the pride of a single goal might ease their pain.

Smiles, tears, and laughter were exchanged, and as we left the hospital we each shook Francois' father's hand, embraced his mother, and promised to return. Anyone would be proud to have parents

THE CHAPEL

Perhaps the only time an entire troop voluntarily attended chapel service was to pray for Francois' full recovery. As Corporal Don Withers said, "There is no such thing as false hope—all hope is true!"

like Mr. and Mrs. Labeau, and although they had not been formally advised, thirty-one recruits had adopted them.

Francois' future career with the RCMP seemed bleak, but we promised never to desert our friend. Never.

One hour later we wandered the streets of Regina. No one had a destination or anything in particular to do. We just wandered. The cool autumn air chilled our near-bald heads, but our freedom from the watchful eye of our instructors felt immense.

"Hey skinhead!" a voice called out from across the street. It came from a group of three local youths. "Heard one of your guys got what you all deserve."

The relationship between RCMP recruits and local youths was deplorable. The locals had always felt threatened. RCMP recruits were well groomed, in good physical condition, and had something few local chaps had—money in their wallets. They saw us as a scourge on their streets. We dated the prettiest girls in town and always had enough money to entertain them.

"What about it, skinhead! Your guy gonna die or what?" the voice called out again.

André Bryant had always impressed us as a calm, in-control sort of guy, but with the last comment a blush came over his face. Then he turned pale. He walked across the street to confront the youths, and we listened as André walked his way into becoming a legend.

"No, our friend ain't gonna die or what," he said.

"Shit. That's too bad. Maybe it's your turn instead." The three individuals encircled André, closing in on him tightly.

"This is not good," Don Outman said as we all began crossing the street.

Before we could make the trek across the road, three of Regina's young citizenry lay motionless on the sidewalk. None of us actually saw what happened. Bryant's moves were too fast and strange to our eyes, but the results were plain to see.

"I think we should head back to the base," André said. "Don't want to be around when they wake up." Nodding our heads in agreement, we turned and left quickly.

"Where in God's name did you learn to fight like that?" Don asked.

"Long story," André replied. "Keep moving."

Thirty minutes later we were sitting on the edges of our beds hoping that Regina City Police would not be paying us a visit. Our first day in Regina had been a day of warnings. We had been warned against going to town without wearing ties, against driving carelessly, and, most important, we had been warned against becoming involved in altercations with the local citizens.

"They see you as a threat and will attempt to single you out. Recruits are a trophy for the locals," Corporal Wheeler had explained. "They want to fight you and they will. It is your duty to avoid a fight at all costs." Then he had added, "But I don't expect any member of this Force to back down. Only one thing you had better remember ..." He had paused as our eyes widened in anticipation. "... if anyone here enters into a fight, you had better not lose or you'll answer to me."

We had not lost this fight.

"What did you do, André?" Lumchuck asked. "I ain't never seen no one fight like that."

"What I did was fail," he replied. "I should have walked away, but when they started talking about Francois ... I just sort of ..." André stopped in mid-sentence. We understood his feelings. We all shared the fear of losing Francois. We also shared the anger André had vented toward the youths who would insult or degrade our friend who was in the hospital, fighting for his life.

We were beginning to understand what Corporal Wheeler had meant when he expressed his hopes that we might "cease being a troop of individuals and become an individual troop."

With Francois in the hospital we were not complete. It was as though a limb had been severed and we were hoping for a re-attachment.

We spent the remainder of the afternoon constructing carefully worded statements that would absolve us of blame in the event the assault was investigated.

Two hours later, supper came and went. More mystery meat accompanied by a side order of pulpy vegetables cooked well beyond the point of mercy.

"Look, the letter 'U'." Lumchuck held up a strip of carrot as he bent it nearly into a circle. "Think this is a carrot, or a sliver of very old turnip?" he asked before cramming it into his mouth. Lumchuck's profound obesity was founded in his ability to eat anything—in large quantities.

"I'm sorry." Phil pushed his plate aside. "Whatever they put in this shepherd's pie isn't meat. The only resemblance it has to meat is its colour." We all tasted the brown, chunky, semi-liquid that flowed out from under the mashed potatoes.

"Tastes like day-old lizard left in the sun to rot," Phil commented.

"Yeah? Well I wouldn't know. Never tasted a day-old, sun-dried lizard," Outman replied.

We laughed.

"Quiet!" Corporal Wheeler had been watching. "How dare you insult this fine dining establishment." He held a tray of food in his hand as he walked to the NCOs' table. "You ought to be ashamed. An army marches on its stomach." He added, "Now eat!" His orders were clear.

Slowly we pulled our trays back in front of us and pushed the brown lumps back under the potatoes. Perhaps if we could hide them ...

Over a month had passed since our first encounter with the "Depot Diner" and we had learned to consume unknown vegetables, jellied critters, deep-fried lumps, and even stew, often containing hair. But tonight was different. The shepherd's pie could not be eaten.

Corporal Wheeler had taken a mouthful and chewed it before looking in our direction. Another chew, another look in our direction, and we knew he had tasted the same unknown flavour that we had encountered. The flavour was unique. Sweet and sour combined with a hint of bitterness. But the smell ...

Raising his paper napkin to his lips, Corporal Wheeler wiped slowly and returned the paper to his tray. It contained a lump that looked like a won ton. He could not swallow the unknown fibrous lump.

Unable to admit defeat, he sampled the vegetables. Although he managed to swallow, we could see it was not an easy task. Moments later he strode up and down between the tables, examining each untouched meal.

"Gonna be a hungry night tonight, lads." Then he turned and walked into the kitchen.

"Oh, to be a fly on that wall," Phil said.

"Shush."

Wheeler had raised his voice to the cook, but no one could make out the content of the conversation. It became obvious that shepherd's pie would be permanently removed from the cook's list of hateful things to do to recruits. For the next week the cook would not make eye contact with us and remained, for the most part, hidden behind the kitchen partition, venturing out only when necessary.

Corporal Wheeler returned, red-faced, and spoke to the mess hall. The acoustics were excellent and clearly we heard him say only one word: "Horsemeat."

Outman coughed a brown lump back onto his plate. Didarski drank his water, then reached over and drank Outman's. Krzyszyk turned his head and grimaced. Together we stood up, returned our near-full plates to the washing racks, and departed.

Except for Lumchuck.

His plate was empty.

Later that night our dormitory speaker played "Lights Out" and we all went to sleep hungry.

Except Lumchuck.

CHAPTER SEVEN
Swimming—A Time to Die

Monday, November 20: November in Saskatchewan was cold. Our troop had been assigned to sweep the parade square of snow, but the prairie wind fought our attempts, covering the asphalt behind us as we swept in vain. Corporal Withers was on duty, watching thirty-one brooms in their unsuccessful attempt at clearing the square. After six passes we stopped.

"What are you giving up for?" he asked.

"Can't seem to make any progress," Didarski replied.

"So what's your point?"

"Well, why continue to try when failure follows so close behind?" Phil looked over his shoulder at the snow that was drifting over the freshly swept parade square.

"So, today we learn that when we are faced with failure, we quit? Is that it? Beaten by a little snowdrift? Poor little boys." Withers placed his hands on his hips and leaned forward. "Poor little lads. You work for twenty minutes then decide to give up." His voice became serious. "I won't have you behaving like that. Not on my parade square. You will continue to sweep the square until it is clean. Breakfast is an option this morning. Fatigue is not an option this morning, and mark my words, lads, failure is not an option this morning!" He shouted his last directions. "I heard late last night that Francois has progressed beyond toe wiggling. He sat up and moved his legs. He didn't give up after twenty minutes. Now, there's a man. Don't you think you owe him a clean parade square?"

Back and forth we swept—infuriated and embarrassed that we had given up so easily. Francois was fighting against doctors who said he would never walk and a priest who had already sent his soul to Heaven. We had been beaten by a few snowflakes.

Like madmen we swept. Back and forth, each time moving the same snow we had just brushed away. Breakfast came and went and we could smell the greasy bacon and half-cooked pancakes.

But still we swept.

Then, as if by magic, the wind ceased and one last pass cleaned the parade square. We stopped, looked at Corporal Withers, then at the black asphalt parade square. We had won. Failure was not an option. We had won.

"Lesson to be learned." Withers spoke loud enough for us all to hear. "Your spirit, your will to win, and the courage to overcome your obstacles are more important than the events that occur around you. This parade square will never be as important as the effort you all put forth to clean it." We nodded in agreement as he added, "The game, gentlemen, goes not to the strong and swift, but to those who keep on playing."

Thirty-one hungry stomachs returned to "B" Block—our dorm, our sanctuary for thirty minutes before our first class of the day.

"That Withers guy sure is weird," Lumchuck said as he retrieved a stash of cookies from his dirty laundry sack. His mother, in an attempt to help maintain his rotund stature, sent five pounds of cookies, date squares, and fudge each week. They nestled safely amongst his dirty socks, shirts, and underwear, where no one would touch them.

"Yeah, some kind of philosopher," Don added.

"Hey, hear what he said about Francois?"

"Think he'll ever finish off his recruit training?"

"Snowflake's chance in hell," Phil called out.

Then the room went quiet as André spoke. "Same chance as we had fighting those million snowflakes that we conquered this morning?" We smiled. "The game, gentlemen, goes not to the strong and the swift, but to those who keep on playing." He mimicked Don Withers' voice as he repeated his message.

"Yeah, some kind of philosopher," Lumchuck repeated.

"Hey Larry, you clean up those cookie crumbs this time, will ya? We got C.B.'d last week because of you."

Harold Burl appeared out of nowhere. Harold never spoke much. He was too insecure to enter into most conversations, but he worried. Harold worried enough to keep our whole troop at ease. Sneaking up behind Lumchuck with a dustpan and whisk, he swept away the crumbs and disappeared through the doors to the trashcan.

"Yeah, Lumchuck. You and your lousy crumbs. We all paid the price."

"Mmmff," Lumchuck replied through a mouthful of chocolate chip cookies.

Like robots we each attended to our pit.

Our weekly dormitory inspections had turned brutal. Corporal

Wheeler made the rounds with Corps Sergeant Major Bilby, inspecting each nook, each crevice, and each surface. When Bilby's white glove picked up even a hint of dust or lint our weekend plans were shattered. A discord had begun in our troop. Each time dust was found in a recruit's pit, the entire troop condemned him. Fights erupted routinely. Two months into our training we faced daily reminders of Don Withers' greeting: "Welcome to hell."

Fifteen minutes later, with the beds made, the sheets ironed, and the floors dusted, thirty-one recruits headed out the door, each carrying under his arm a towel and swimming trunks. Our first class of the day was a double tour of duty in the swimming pool.

Everywhere we went on base, we marched as a troop. When in a hurry we "double-timed" our steps. Marching became running, and even when running, our steps had to hit the pavement as one. Individuality was not allowed.

One troop—one step.

Earlier in the week, Lumchuck had tripped and fallen while the troop carried on. Seeing this, Corporal Wheeler had taken away our Friday-night pass. "Everything you do, you will do as an individual troop," he commanded, and we spent that particular Friday night in the typing hall typing his command. One hundred times for each recruit. It was as if they expected repetition to alter our thinking.

They were right.

We had thought about Lumchuck's fall and Wheeler's response and had planned our revenge. A small group of tourists watched as we double-timed our way across the parade square toward the pool. Corporal Wheeler, his boots gleaming so brightly that even the snowflakes were afraid to alight on them, watched and explained to the tourists, with pride, how well he had trained us. As we passed the group, Don Outman slid his foot forward and tripped Lumchuck, who landed hard, like a sack of wet cookies.

"Troop!" someone shouted. Thirty-one recruits fell to the ground. Quickly everyone stood up, dusted the snow from their pants, and continued their run to the swimming pool.

"Bloody spastics," Wheeler said as he walked away from his audience.

We had won. Our collective tumble could not officially be punished, but our collective statement to our Drill Corporal would not be without consequence.

And it would not be pleasant. Corporal Wheeler would ride us harder than any troop. From that day forth, each drill practice would be a tortuous, painful journey toward perfection.

Ten minutes after our fall in the snow, we had changed into our swimming trunks and were standing in the shower. Showers were mandatory before and after swimming class.

"Only clean bodies will enter my pool." It was an order made clear by our swimming instructor, Corporal Thain. "And only clean bodies will leave it."

Corporal Thain was a different sort of individual. Some thought him mad while others reflected on the possibility that he was perverted. Still others merely mused that his mother had dropped him on his head before his skull had hardened. The majority, however, just thought him strange.

Corporal Thain introduced us to the word "freakin'" during our first swimming class, and he used it continuously.

"Hey you in the freakin' showers," he yelled at us. "You got a freakin' party goin' on in there or you just playing hide the soap?" Thain often stood at the open doorway to the shower room. Staring. Sixteen rusty water nozzles made it mandatory for the recruits to stand close while showering, and standing close to another nude male was not a comfortable sensation for a man. Most of the time Thain would watch us in silence. On other occasions he would comment on our physical condition, appearance, and stature. At times his comments were very personal. Too personal.

But Thain was a hygiene fanatic and today was no different. Holding up a recruit's undershorts on his leather riding crop, he screamed into the showers.

"Freakin' tobacco stains!" Our eyes widened. "Freakin' skid marks!" We stood motionless. "Who owns these despicable, contemptible, vile shorts?"

Lumchuck stepped forward.

"I will be sending these freakin' shorts to the Corps Sergeant Major. I am sure he will be duly impressed. You will be in his office at noon today—and Lumchuck," he added, "forget about having any freakin' lunch. I have other plans for you." Larry's lower lip quivered. His cookie stash would not last until the end of the week.

Corporal Thain routinely went through our underwear while we were showering. Some thought it was his duty. Most of us thought otherwise. But clearly, tobacco stains were not allowed.

We left the showers, dressed in our bathing suits, and lined up at the entrance to the pool. Our single-file line took us by two glass doors. We were still wet from the showers, and as we stood on the cold concrete floor, Corporal Thain paused, opened the doors, and drew in a fresh breath of air.

"Freakin' refreshing, isn't it?" The near-zero wind blew by us as we shivered. It was a ritual that he would repeat at the beginning of each swimming class for the duration of our training. With the door wide open and the winter wind whistling by our still-wet bodies, he would proudly proclaim, "When I say stand at attention, I even want to see your nipples looking skyward."

Our nipples obeyed.

Ahead of us waited the pool. It was rumoured that Freakin' Thain imported Arctic ice to keep it cold. The truth was that the heater rarely worked. The pool was in pathetic condition. A thick scum encrusted the water line, tiles were missing, and the water was seldom heated. The only living creature that could survive this environment was the human papilloma virus—the wart virus that grew in the cracks of the pool deck. The pool leaked and was never maintained at a safe or even hygienic condition. Several months after our troop graduated, a member of the RCMP would lose his life when an electrical short in the underwater pool lights reached out through the cold water and stopped his heart.

The pool was our own private hell, where Corporal Thain would teach us to swim and save lives. "Thain," he often said, "rhymes with pain, and that is what I am here to help you overcome."

We could never understand the logic behind his statement. He carried an eight-foot bamboo cane, supposedly to reach out to assist a struggling swimmer. Unfortunately, the pole never served that purpose. It was an instrument of torture whereby he would thrash any recruit whose swimming style and form did not meet his standard.

We had not spent a lot of time in the pool. Most of our lessons were spent lying on the deck, practising swimming form, and when it moved him, Thain would have us strengthen our muscles through the torturous repetitions of "ins and outs." For thirty minutes, the troop would be ordered to jump in the pool and climb out over the deck. No ladders or stairs were allowed. The exercise was devious and painful, but it served its purpose. It gave Thain the dominance he sought.

Lining up on the pool deck, we stood, still shivering, wondering what painful lesson he would teach today. Our wait was short.

"Today you will begin your first lifesaving lesson," he announced.

"And it will be a real freakin' life you will save. Lumchuck," he shouted, "climb the ladder to the high diving platform. Don't worry, lad, I won't make you do anything harmful."

Larry's eyes widened like saucers. He was a nonswimmer and had spent his entire life developing a fear of the water. There had not been a great opportunity to learn to swim in his home town of Edmonton, and his total lack of grace in the water reminded us of a floundering white beluga whale.

"Burl, you follow him up the freakin' ladder." Harold Burl did as directed. The same small group of tourists that had watched us stumble and fall earlier had now collected in the warmth of the upper observation gallery and was eagerly watching the lesson unfold.

As he stood at the edge of the platform, Lumchuck's toes could be seen to lock tight on the edge. Ten little piggies gripping for dear life.

"Burl!" Thain screamed. "Push him in!"

"But ..." Harold looked down at Corporal Thain.

"Are you freakin' deaf, lad? I said push him in. You push him in or I'll shove this pole up your butt until you look like a popsicle, then I'll freakin'-well push you in myself."

"Sorry, Larry," we heard Harold say. "I got no choice."

Larry Lumchuck's body plummeted fifteen feet to the water. Arms and legs flailed as his airborne carcass accelerated downward, and a sickening smack followed as he hit the water and disappeared below the surface.

"One, two, three, four, five—he should be up in about another five seconds," Corporal Thain said.

"Think he's okay, Corporal?" André asked.

"Abso-freakin'-positively," Thain answered. He had a habit of hyphenating words to maintain his quota of the use of the word.

As if on command, the beluga whale surfaced for air.

"Tell me your name," Thain shouted to Lumchuck, but Larry was too busy trying to breathe.

"I said tell me your name, Lumchuck. Tell me your name if you want this." He held the bamboo pole out a few inches away from Lumchuck, teasing him. The spectators leaned forward over the railing.

"Tell me your name, you freakin' coward."

Lumchuck began to cough and sputter.

"Okay, you want the cane?" Thain sneered at his victim.

Larry did not respond. All his energy was being consumed in an attempt to survive.

"You want the cane? Here it is." In one move, Corporal Thain raised the cane high over Lumchuck's head and pulled it down. The tip glanced off his temple, and blood flowed freely into the water. High overhead a combined gasp issued forth from the spectators and from somewhere a faint voice could be heard. "Dat man is crazy."

"Burl," Thain called up to the high platform. "Jump in and rescue him. He's bleeding and I don't want to attract sharks." Harold leapt from the diving platform, and within seconds we helped pull Larry's semiconscious body over the edge of the pool deck.

"You freakin' sissy!" Thain screamed at Lumchuck. Larry's eyes were beginning to open. "You freakin' no-good yellowbelly!" he screamed, adding to the insult. "The only reason I didn't let you freakin'-well drown is that you might make it to Heaven and even God don't want non-swimming wimps in His place."

Deep within the small crowd of tourists, a nun blushed, frowned, then turned her back on the pool.

"Corporal, there's ..." Phil pointed up to the observation gallery, hoping to quietly alert Thain of our holy guest.

"I don't freakin' care," he said, looking up at the tourists. "This is my pool, you are my students, and you will freakin'-well learn to swim and save lives or you'll freakin'-well die learning how."

Then he added in an even louder voice, "Do I make myself freakin' clear?"

"Yes, Corporal."

Lumchuck stood up and glanced toward the glass door leading from the pool to the gymnasium. His face regained its colour, partly due to the blood that was streaming down his forehead and partly because of what he saw.

"Corporal," Larry called out. "Permission to try that again?"

"You freakin' crazy?" Thain replied.

"No, Corporal." Larry smiled at the door. "And I ain't no wimp either."

Not waiting for permission, the beluga climbed the ladder, nodded to the tourists, walked to the edge of the platform, and jumped feet-first into the pool. Surfacing, he called out, "My name is Constable Larry Lumchuck, I am a member of the Royal Canadian Mounted Police, and I just love this freakin' pool."

The troop and the spectators burst into laughter as Thain held out the tip of the cane for him to grasp. "Here, you want it—take it," he said as he released the cane. Lumchuck swam three feet to the far side of the pool, ignored the cane, and glanced again at the glass door. He was smiling.

For the next two hours we practised saving each other's lives. Recruits towed each other back and forth amidst mock struggles to survive. We swam underwater, surfacing behind our make-believe victims in order to grasp them safely, and we pulled each other over the pool deck until our chests bled from the abrasive concrete.

"Lovely. Just abso-freakin'-positively lovely." Corporal Thain could not believe his eyes.

Lumchuck had given us all the courage to go on—to push ourselves beyond our own fears. But what had Larry seen to inspire him? Something had kindled a fire within our fat friend and that fire had burned in our hearts for two hours.

What had he seen through those glass doors?

As our two-hour marathon swimming and life-saving lesson came to a close, Corporal Thain turned to us and spoke. Shivering, we listened. "You're still a bunch of useless freakin' cretins, but you've started something today. At least one of you will be called upon during your career to jump into cold water and save a life. When that happens, you will discover that there is no next time, no second chance, no time out. When that happens, time will stand still and you will either save a life or spend the rest of yours in shame." Quietly he added, "There is no such thing as bravery in our police force. The day you join, the day you take those three oaths, that is true bravery. Everything else is what I expect of you."

Silence.

"Class dismissed."

Back in the showers, the hot water loosened our tongues and we spoke. "Did you notice he didn't say freakin' at the end of the class?"

"Yeah."

"Hey that was some class, wasn't it?"

"Freakin' wonderful."

"Hey Larry, you okay?"

"Freakin' okay, buddy," Larry replied and smiled. "I think I might give up those cookies. They're weighing me down."

"Lumpy," Outman called out. Larry Lumchuck's protruding stomach had given him a new nickname. "What did you see through that door? We couldn't get an angle on it."

"Wait for it," Larry replied, poking his head out of the shower room.

DEPOT SWIMMING POOL

The pool (circa 1967) has been closed for many years, but if one were to enter the building late at night and stand still, the faint echo of a bamboo cane striking flesh might still be heard.

"Hey guys, you got room in dat shower for a wheelchair?" a familiar voice called out.

Our mouths fell open and thirty-one nude males stared at the open shower-room doorway. There, in a wheelchair, an old friend sat watching us as we stood, motionless, in silent astonishment. Then the steamy room exploded.

"Francois!" thirty-one voices screamed. "Francois!"

We set a record for drying and dressing that day. We had a thousand questions for our troopmate and could hardly wait for answers.

In the locker room, Francois told us he had been released from the hospital early that morning. He had been aware that we knew he was progressing, but he had wanted to keep his return to the troop a secret because he hadn't been sure he would have the strength to fulfil his dream. His parents had returned to Montreal that morning and he had been given permission to return to training, if only to partake in the academic studies. His future with the RCMP was still in doubt, but as far as we were concerned, Francois was home.

The remainder of the day went by quickly. Francois would not allow his wheelchair to be pushed. He was too proud. He would be allowed to use the service elevator in our barracks, but otherwise he would take no special privileges as he rejoined our troop. His dignity would not allow any special treatment. He followed behind the troop at first, then later he took the lead as we "forward harched" behind the man who had shown us courage.

From that day on, as the command "Forward harch!" was given, one voice in the troop could be heard to say, "Forward wheel!"

Later that night we sat and listened to our friend tell of his recovery. He explained that two weeks prior to his release from the hospital, the medical staff had advised him that he might never walk again. Fortunately, Don Withers had visited him that evening and reminded him that doctors often make mistakes.

"He told me dat if I wanted to succeed, all I had to give was everything dat I had. Dat night I stopped crying and did my first sit-up. Boy did dat ever hurt." We all laughed, and he continued his story of sit-ups, push-ups, and toe wiggles. Tears came to his eyes when the subject of his graduation was mentioned. No one knew if he would ever walk again, but we encouraged him and vowed to give him our strength.

"Failure is not an option," Don Outman reminded him. "You'll graduate with us or we'll all stay behind."

Later that night, just before "lights out," Larry passed the remainder of his cookies to his troopmates as he borrowed from the courage that Francois had exhibited. "I'm gonna lose weight," he said. "Some day, Francois, I want to be just as good as you."

Shortly afterwards, as the dormitory speakers played their scratchy tune, our lights went out and we slept.

And no one cried.

"Laws are like a spider's web. They catch the weak and the foolish, while allowing the bigger, wealthier, and stronger to break free."

Corporal Dunsel

CHAPTER EIGHT
Law Class—Just Another Homicide

Tuesday, December 19: We were halfway through our training and Christmas was closing in fast. We had all been promised a five-day pass to return home to visit our families. In preparation, all our written assignments had been completed and our boots had received an extra coat of polish. The threat of being confined to barracks loomed heavy over our heads. One speck of lint, one scratch on a spit-shone boot, or one written assignment not completed could deny us a Christmas homecoming and destroy our holiday.

In an effort to ensure his Christmas pass, Lumchuck had lost fifteen pounds. Francois had served as his mentor. After many hours talking together, Larry had come to understand that his dreams of success were nothing without the courage to make them come true. Francois had taught him this simple truism, and daily they rehearsed it. Each night in our barracks, Francois wiggled his toes and smiled as he sensed some small personal gain. But it was not just Francois who enjoyed nightly success. Lumchuck, in his constant battle of the bulge, dispensed his mother's cookies around the room. A sense of unity and pride had taken control of our troop. Each noonday parade we would march behind the senior troop. Staring straight ahead, we could see only the backs of their scarlet tunics, which were symbols of their success—not ours.

Pride drove us forward. Larry lost weight and Francois increased his toe wiggling; we all fought to better ourselves.

Every night while Lumchuck awarded each of us a sacred cookie, Francois disappeared with André Bryant. An hour later they returned as mysteriously as they had vanished. We developed a nightly ritual after lights-out. Someone would thank Lumchuck for his cookie and we would all shout a small "Thanks, Larry!" Then, in the darkness, someone would ask, "Where'd you go tonight, Francois?"

The only reply was an occasional "Ask André."

Just as our evenings ended predictably, our mornings began alike—at 0700 hours. Breakfast time at the legendary mess.

I sat beside Francois and watched as he slid his bacon over his pancakes. Looking at the glutinous diskscovered with shredded swine flesh in front of us, I whispered, "Now I know why they call this place a mess."

"I just hate it when dey put de two uncooked sides togedder," André said. "I tink it is like glue and I can't get dem apart."

"Don't try," I suggested. "You don't really want to see what's in them anyway."

Speaking at the meal table was not allowed, but in hushed voices we told Francois about the horsemeat shepherd's pie and the other culinary delights he had missed during his sojourn in the hospital.

"RCMP. It stands for Rotten Crappy Mouldy Pancakes," a voice offered.

"No, try Reptile Creamed Mashed Potatoes," still another voice suggested.

"Rotten Cadaver Meat Pie." We chuckled as the acronyms kept coming. It took our minds away from our food. It made swallowing easier.

"How's it goin', Francois," I said softly, wondering how he maintained his brave front.

"I tink it is good. Dat André sure is helping a lot. He says I got nerves to bring to life and he keeps pinching me. Boy dat hurts some time, but last night I got a big jerk."

"Big jerk?"

"Oui. He pinch me on de knee, and my foot, she flew up. It hurt like hell but den he says it is good. My legs are not dead."

André Bryant remained inscrutable. He never mentioned his past and spoke of his home only as "back east." He preached "calm, courage, and confidence" to us all, and he possessed the same inner wisdom I had come to respect in Corporal Don Withers. Yet his nightly escape with Francois kept the rest of us guessing. We had questioned both of them, but still no one knew where they went or what they were doing. When they returned, Francois would be covered with sweat and André would be smiling. On occasion we would find Francois' wheelchair in the stairwell—empty.

"Ask Francois," André would reply to our interrogations.

"Ask André," Francois would reply. But he smiled when we showed interest. Whatever was happening agreed with our wheelchair-bound friend.

"Don't know how you're doing it, Francois. You seem to be putting weight on that skinny frame of yours. Sure isn't the pancakes they serve, is it?" I asked.

"Ask André," he replied, and we both burst out laughing. Francois' increasing upper body mass was indeed a mystery to everyone, except Francois. And André Bryant. It seemed near impossible to build muscle on our diet, which was fat-rich, protein-poor, and bland. Yet Francois was being transformed—it was no illusion.

"Troop!" A voice announced the arrival of Corps Sergeant Major Bilby. We sat at attention, our arms held rigid and vertical by our sides.

"Good morning," he said. "Any complaints or suggestions regarding the food?"

"No, sir," a trained voice rang out. "Excellent dining facility we have here."

"Good. The way to a man's heart is through his stomach," he said, then turned to leave.

"Not if you're a colorectal specialist," a hushed voice replied.

CSM Bilby stopped, turned, raised one eyebrow, then spoke. "If you have any complaints, report them to my office in person."

No complaints were registered. Larry Lumchuck and Harold Burl had tried that during our first month in training. As a reward they peeled potatoes every night for two weeks.

Moments later dishes clattered and silverware tinkled as we deposited our trays in the dish rack and headed off for our first class of the day: Criminal Law.

Ten minutes later, thirty-two men sat in a small sweaty-smelling classroom, patiently awaiting the most boring subject taught at the training academy.

Corporal Dunsel entered the room and stood at the head of the class. As our law instructor, he knew it all. We knew that to be true because he had told us so. Corporal Dunsel had first-hand experience with legal prosecutions. As a twenty-year veteran of the Force, he had not only arrested many suspects, but also possessed the unique experience of having been arrested himself.

One conviction for impaired driving had resulted in his driver's licence being suspended. Automatically, that meant a transfer to an administrative position: law instructor.

Corporal Dunsel was not our most inspiring instructor, but he often added colour to his lessons. Criminal Law was a dull subject, made palatable only by Dunsel's creativity and humour. If his humour failed to keep us awake, there was always punishment. Rumours of his past were commonplace amongst recruits. We had heard that his transfer to the academy was a punitive move. We later learned that, considering his lacklustre career, he was indeed fortunate to even retain his rank and employment with the Force.

But he was our law instructor and we were his students. We sat captive. There were no choices to be made. He would talk and we would take notes.

Although sometimes boring, Corporal Dunsel was famous for his theatrics. His law lectures involved the liberal display of handcuffs and riot batons. When he taught "legal use of force" he would demonstrate, usually on poor Larry Lumchuck. In the short three months we had been students in the academy, Larry's arrest record surpassed that of even the most hardened criminal. He had been arrested for possessing too many pounds, snorting while laughing, and even falling asleep in class. Many times, poor Lumchuck, after having been "read his rights," was forced to sit through law class handcuffed, with a warrant for his arrest taped securely to his shirt. The ridicule, however, served a purpose. With each infraction we would learn a new technique of handcuffing, a new wrinkle in the administration of justice or the detaining of a suspect.

Although his discipline record matched Lumchuck's class arrest record, Corporal Dunsel taught us not just criminal law, but also its practical application.

"Each class I teach will be backed by experience," he would often proclaim. Frequently he would add, "It is a smart man who learns from his own mistakes—but a wise man who learns from the mistakes of others. Learn from my mistakes, lads, and you will not be condemned to repeat them." His comments confirmed the rumours we had heard. He had made many mistakes.

Although we learned well under this instructor's guidance, we could not have prepared ourselves for one lesson. Standing at the head of the class, Corporal Dunsel spoke clearly and loudly. "Today, lads, I will not be arresting Lumchuck for his fattitude, nor will I detain Constable Didarski for possession of an oversized ear. No, Teather, I will not cite you for that cheesy moustache you are trying to cultivate under that big honkin' nose of yours. Today's lesson will be on principles and ethics."

AN INDIVIDUAL TROOP

(Troop 18, November 1967) When one member of the troop was in need of "encouragement" he would be tied to a chair, given a cold shower, and "encouraged to try harder." This technique was often successfully used to "adjust attitudes."

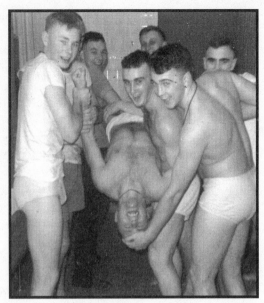

Ethics was a topic Corporal Dunsel had never addressed before. We had often thought it was because he had little experience.

"Lumchuck, listen up. Didarski, cock that big ear in my direction, and Labeau, if I catch you slouching in that wheelie chair of yours I'm gonna make you stand in the corner for the entire period."

"Dat would be fine wit me, if I could," Francois replied.

"Shut up, Labeau. If I want any shit out of you, I'll squeeze your head."

"Yes, Caporal." Francois sat up straight. He sat at the rear of the lecture hall, but his attention was clearly focussed on our instructor.

"Listen carefully, lads. For the next hour I forbid you to leave your chairs, to move, to speak, or even to think, unless I order it. Is that clear?" A collective head nod acknowledged the order. "Soon, should you possess the wisdom and strength to graduate from this academy, you will be given more power than anyone in this free country. You will be given the power to take away from all men that which we cherish most."

Dunsel's eyes looked down at the floor and we wondered if he was recalling the night he was arrested for impaired driving.

"Freedom," he said, in a voice that commanded respect. "You are the only people in our wonderful country who can take away freedom. Politicians cannot pull people from their houses or their cars and lock them up. Doctors cannot summarily order a person into a hospital, and even lawyers, unless they are terribly inadequate, cannot imprison their clients. You will be given authority above and beyond your government, and you will be trained, armed, and trusted to carry out this duty.

"There will be few checks and balances to control you, and what happens between you and an obnoxious drunk in a back alley will be a matter between you, him, and your God." Dunsel paused, drew a deep breath, and continued. "Today I want you to understand the dignity and the enormity of this power ... this responsibility that you will accept. Power is the ultimate aphrodisiac, and I fear it will drive a few of you to your own abusive orgy. Your power is immense, lads, and the greater the power, the more dangerous the abuse—and ..." He paused for a moment, then continued. "... a few of you will abuse it. Will it be you, Lumchuck? How about you, Outman? Lots of dark prairie roads out there. Only you and the next impaired driver you arrest. Didarski, what about you? What are you gonna do the next time someone calls you flap-ear? Teather? Those rosy-red white-tipped pimples on your forehead are a perfect target. Whatchya gonna do when some drunk calls you zit-head?"

My eyes looked down at my notes. I was embarrassed. I had hoped my teenage acne would leave, but even at the age of twenty, it remained.

"Francois?" he continued. "If you ever climb out of that wheelchair, how are you going to respond when a drunk calls you Frog? Shut up. I don't want to hear any answers because none of you know yet."

We wondered where this lesson was heading, but we sat in silence as he went on.

"You have the power to arrest anyone whom you find committing a criminal offence. That, lads, is the extent of your power. You can exercise your power to save a life, to protect society, or to engage in ..."

CRASH!

The door at the rear of the classroom flew open.

"Bastard! You bastard!" a voice shouted. We watched in shock as a masked individual crashed through the door, nearly taking it off its hinge.

"Bastard!" he shouted again. "I told you to stay away from my wife and now I find out ..." The unidentified man pulled a small gun from his belt as he ran to the front of the class. Shots were fired, and Corporal Dunsel's body slammed backwards against the wall. His eyes were wide with shock and his body retched as he coughed. Blood spewed from his mouth and dotted several faces in the front row. Slowly he slid to the floor as the assailant turned, ran between our seats, and left through the same door by which he had entered.

Labeau spun his wheelchair ninety degrees and caught the aggressor's shin with his foot rest.

"Shit!" the unknown aggressor yelled as he grabbed his ankle. Briefly he pointed his gun at Labeau's face, then he reached out, grasped one of the handles attached to the chair's backrest, and flung the chair and Francois to the ground. Francois hit the floor hard, his arms flailing and reaching out for anything to break his fall.

"Bastard!" was the last word we heard as he left the room.

Corporal Dunsel's past had caught up with him and justice had been administered summarily. His body remained motionless on the floor, and thirty-two would-be police officers sat frozen with fear.

"Let's get him!" Outman yelled as he ran to the back of the room. We rose to our feet at once, following in his footsteps.

"Freeze!" a familiar voice commanded. "I said, freeze!"

Corporal Dunsel rose to his feet and wiped the red liquid from his chin. The blood was fake. "They call me Lazarus Man," he said as he smiled and began to laugh. "I will give you all five minutes to write, in statement form, everything that you observed. Yes, this was a set-up, a plot, a scam, a charade arranged just for you. Everything you have heard about me since the day you arrived was conveyed just for today. Just for this hour. I was not transferred to Depot because of an impaired driving charge nor am I the immoral degenerate that I have been rumoured to be." He smiled wide, revealing red-stained teeth. "I am Lazarus Man, rising from the dead to test your powers of observation. Lads, take your pencils in hand and write down what you have seen. You will not talk about this to each other. I want your observations only."

For five minutes we wrote our stories, each based on our own private realities. Some saw the assailant as a big, heavy-set man wearing a plaid shirt and blue jeans. Others saw him as possessing an average build and wearing a mackinaw jacket and a cowboy hat. Still others saw only the gun—big and black.

For the next fifty minutes, we read our statements aloud to the class. Astoundingly, our stories were very similar, although lacking in enough detail to qualify us to be good court witnesses.

"Labeau?" Dunsel called. "You're the last one. What did you see?"

Francois looked down at his statement and read. Our eyes widened in amazement as his detailed account was delivered.

"At oh eight hundred hours de rear door to de classroom was kicked open. An adult male yelled 'bastard' twice and told you to stay away from his wife. He fired two shots into your chest at a distance of about five feet, den turned and left. He was wearing a plaid shirt and blue jeans and his name was Caporal Ronald Wederspoon. If you like, I have a photo of him—without de stocking on his face."

"Huh?" Dunsel replied. "What makes you so sure about all this and who the hell is Corporal Weatherspoon?"

"I don't know, Caporal, never seen dat man before."

"How'd you know he kicked the door open? He could have pushed it. That simple piece of testimony in court could give you problems."

"Not if we photograph his footprint on de outside of dat door, Caporal. It wasn't dere when we entered de class dis morning."

"Corporal Weatherspoon?" Dunsel faked ignorance.

"Well, as he pulled me out of my chair, I tink I tore his back pocket. I got dis souvenir." Labeau held up a brown leather wallet as he opened it to reveal a police badge and photographic identification.

"Prove it was his and not stolen. You're assuming a lot, aren't you?"

Looking down at the steel footrest of his wheelchair, Labeau spoke. "I tink we heard about DNA evidence from you last week, Caporal?"

"Yes. DNA testing is still in its infancy, but it shows a lot of promise."

"Well, I got some blood on my wheelchair and I tink some fibres also."

"Labeau, you done good!" Dunsel exclaimed. "But how did you get all of this into that tiny little crippled French brain of yours?"

"When you can only sit, you get to see a lot," Francois reported, "and I see by de repairs on dat hinge," he pointed toward the door, "dat dis isn't de first time you been shot."

The troop exploded into laughter.

Lazarus Man indeed.

"You did well, Francois." Dunsel acknowledged Labeau's enhanced powers of observation. "As for the rest of you, if you ever sit paralyzed when something like this happens again, I'll personally come gunning for you, and my revolver won't contain blanks."

"But you told us not to leave our chairs, Corporal." Didarski stroked his smaller ear, offering an excuse for our inaction.

"Never obey an order if it conflicts with your sworn duty! Do I make myself clear?" Dunsel shouted. "I said, do I make myself bloody well clear?"

"Yes, Corporal." Thirty-two voices acknowledged his order.

"So, my lesson to you today is threefold. One ..." He paused, holding up the index finger of his right hand. "The power of a police officer can be summarily executed and supersedes any civilian's authority. Upon graduation, you will all possess this awesome power. Exercise it well, lads."

A second finger appeared beside his forefinger. "Two! You must be prepared at all times to observe and record everything you see and hear."

Then he raised his third finger and softened his address. "Three. Your duty, your responsibility, and your power as a police officer must never be diluted, weakened, or bastardized by anyone. You as police officers must remain free to exercise your duty and responsibility so that the citizens of our country may be free to exercise their freedom."

The class was quiet.

"Class dismissed."

We stood and turned toward the door. The law lecture had been a ruse. The preliminary insults served to catch us off guard and to disguise the real test. Corporal Dunsel was not the failure we thought him to be, but the rumour was deep into our collective consciousness and we vowed to maintain it—for his next troop.

"Oh, Labeau, throw me the wallet. I think Corporal Weatherspoon would like it back."

As the brown leather wallet arced over our heads, we caught a glimpse of the metal badge it contained.

"Some day I'll wear one of dem," Francois said as he pushed hard on his wheels and followed us out the door.

"Some day you will, lad." Corporal Dunsel's voice came from behind. "Some day you will."

> "The fault is great in any Mountie
> Who steals and eats forbidden bounty,
> Yet steal we did—we drank and ate.
> Inspector Chicken sealed our fate."
> —Troop 18 (composed atop an elevator shaft)

CHAPTER NINE
The Ninjas of Troop 18—Stolen Food and Lost Friends

Wednesday, January 3: Christmas had come and gone. It was a bitter time for our troop. Everyone had gone home to celebrate Christmas with their families.

Everyone except Francois and André.

Francois could not face the indignity of boarding an airplane using his wheelchair, and André quietly proclaimed that he "really had no home." Together they had remained at Depot, enjoying bacon and pancakes and other mixed-grill delights served up by a skeleton crew at the mess.

It was dark when my return flight arrived at Regina airport. The night seemed even colder than the minus ten degrees Fahrenheit registered on the airport television-screen monitor. It was dark and cold. And lonely.

Christmas had been an emotional roller coaster that I had ridden for the few days I had spent at home. As I was soon to learn, I was not alone.

My parents looked on me curiously. Their eyes said I was different. My father said that I had changed, but when questioned he was evasive, and I was left wondering whether or not he approved of the changes he perceived. Only three friends openly accepted the changes the RCMP had inflicted upon me.

Loyal Burke, a retired magician with whom I had developed a brotherhood, came to our house, taught me a few new magic tricks, then shook my hand as he left. On our front porch, in the cold winter air, he looked deep into my eyes. I will not forget his parting words. "Your journey is just begun and mine is near an end. I have taught you how to palm a coin and how to levitate small objects, but you will have to discover true magic for yourself." My eyes filled with tears as this old friend waved, then walked away. In the short two years I had known him, he had shown me true magic—the magic of friendship. Nothing had changed that—we were still friends. One year later, news of Loyal's death would strike a blow to my soul.

Another friend, my schoolmate Brian Zimmerman, was studying to become a schoolteacher. In the few brief hours we spent together, we joked freely about how I would deal with his failures. Brian would remain a lifelong friend, and thirty years later our friendship would still remain as a shining example of the true magic that Loyal had stood for.

Then there was Ben. Ben and I had grown up together. He lived across the street from our house, and together we had discovered mud pies, butterflies, and puberty. Ben and I had been inseparable. We had known each other's thoughts, wishes, and secrets and had often spoken of the day when we would grow up and leave each other. Neither of us knew then of the pain that lay ahead.

When I had left home, Ben weighed over 170 pounds and stood nearly six feet tall. During my Christmas vacation I visited him in the hospital. He weighed less than one hundred pounds. Ben was dying of cancer.

I had been ordered by my parents not to discuss Ben's impending death. He had never been told that his cancer was terminal. Even his parents had elected not to reveal his future. As I sat beside Ben's bed, I remembered the lesson that Corporal Dunsel had taught. I remembered his words clearly: "Never obey an order if it conflicts with your sworn duty."

I had a duty and it was one of friendship, trust, and truth. Together, Ben and I talked. We both knew he was dying, and I shared his sadness that his parents opted not to talk truthfully with him. Ben was wise beyond his years; he recognized that it wasn't mistrust that kept his parents from confiding in him—it was fear.

That afternoon, Ben and I shared time, space, and friendship. Then we said goodbye.

As I sat in the Regina airport waiting for a taxi, Ben's last words still played back inside my head.

"Don't worry, Bob. I know where I'm going. Guess I got one up on you."

"Where you going, Ben?" I asked.

"Home."

Neither Ben nor I cried. Instead, we talked, we laughed, and for a while we sat silently. In a quiet moment, Ben and I had forgiven our parents for their inability to deal with his illness.

Perhaps it was because we were both young, perhaps it was because we were close friends, but dealing with death was, for both of us, a strangely personal experience—an experience that I have long treasured. As I left his hospital room, he smiled, waved, and I heard him say through a set of vocal cords nearly burned out with radiation, "Goin' home. Take care, ol' buddy."

"Goodbye, Ben. Goodbye, my friend."

Damn, I hated leaving you, Ben.

"Taxi?" a voice called out.

Fifteen minutes later I walked into the barracks. My stomach was hollow, and I envied the friend I had left behind. He had a home to go to.

Eight members of the troop were sitting quietly in the dormitory when I arrived. There wasn't much conversation. Didarski sat on the edge of his bed, holding his hand over his mouth.

"Whatsa matter, Phil?" I asked.

"Outman. The creep hit me." An argument over the ownership of a cigar had resulted in a fight. Fights amongst members of the same troop were usually interrupted by the other troopmates. When this was not possible, the outcome was often savage. Our self-defence instructor taught us never to give up unless dead or unconscious, and

DEPOT IN THE WINTER (CIRCA 1967)

The loneliest place on earth is said to be the RCMP Training Academy during the first few days after Christmas break.

this fight had seen Phil Didarski lying on the ground unconscious.

Across the dorm, Don Outman sat, smiling, blowing cigar smoke in our direction. "Here, I believe this is yours?" Outman opened his outstretched hand, revealing a half-tooth fresh from the mouth of his troopmate. Then he took us both off guard.

"Phil," he said as he stood up and approached Didarski's pit, "sorry 'bout your girlfriend. I didn't know, and an hour ago I didn't care. Seems all my friends have changed too. That cigar was the only thing I had to look forward to when I returned here."

"Aw, fschucks." Phil winced with the pain. "It'fs okay. I needed a new toof anyway. This one broke too easy."

Together we laughed. Phil nearly cried in pain with every inhalation. Cool air drove the nerve to send a pain message directly to his brain, and every time he laughed he covered his mouth until his cheeks would fill out and his laughs exited through his nostrils.

As the night wore on we learned a horrible truth. Too many of our troopmates had lost their girlfriends and fiancées, and poor Phil Didarski had lost his "only true love."

"And I loft my freakin' toof too!" he added. His comment sounded humorous, but his tears told a different story.

André Bryant and Francois Labeau were there to receive us. Although only six recruits had arrived, we discovered we had all experienced the same holiday. We compared stories, speaking of old friends who no longer recognized us and of parents who said that we had changed—somehow.

In our common friendship, none of us understood how we had changed, and no one really cared. We had each other.

And we shared a common ground. We were troopmates.

It was nearing midnight. There would be no classes tomorrow. Many of the instructors were still on holidays, allowing the recruits an extra day of leisure.

"Cheeze I'm hungry," Don Outman said.

"Yeah, me too," came another hungry voice.

"Haven't eaten for centuries." André added, "I think I could even eat some pancakes and bacon."

"Give your head a shake," someone replied.

The mess was closed and the vending machine had emptied its sugar cargo and had never been refilled. In the midst of the RCMP Academy, we sat—starving.

"Well, there is food to be found," André said.

"Yeah right. Whatchya gonna do, rip open the sticky-bun machine and lick the inside walls?"

"We could send out for pizza."

"Nothing open this late."

"There is food to be found," André repeated quietly.

"Where?" I asked.

"Remember the shift we spent together last week?" he asked. "We worked Night Guard patrol from midnight until reveille."

"Yes."

"Remember when I went missing for an hour?"

"Yes, you never did tell me where you went."

"You men still hungry?"

"Yes, Constable," we all replied in unison, mocking the collective voice we had used daily in the presence of our instructors.

"Then let's get us some food."

"Where?"

"You must follow my instructions," André said. "First order of the day is dress."

"Dress?"

"Dress. Put on the darkest clothes you have."

"Is this Ninja shit?" Don Outman asked. In a rare revealing moment several weeks ago, André had confided that he had studied the art of Ninjitsu for several years. Despite this revelation, most of his past was still unknown to us.

"Sort of, but we'll just call it foraging," André answered. "We're goin' on a hunt."

Within five minutes we were dressed in browns, blacks, and greys.

"Francois, dress warm, you're running interference for us."

"I can do dat," Francois replied.

"At midnight—precisely—you will sit in your wheelchair, outside the mess. We will need ten minutes. Should any instructor, any recruit, any person at all attempt entry into the mess, fall out of your chair, groan, flip around in the snow, and do anything you can to give us ten minutes. Then get your crippled butt back here for the feast."

"I can do dat."

"The mess? How we gonna get into the mess?" Outman asked. "It's locked up tighter than a bull's arse in fly season."

André outlined his plan. While on Night Guard duty, he had discovered an entrance to the underground tunnels that crisscrossed the base. A central heating plant located on the complex sent out a system of steam pipes to every building. The tunnels containing the pipes measured about four feet wide and five feet tall. These shafts led to each house, each barrack building, the gymnasium, the classrooms, and to our goal: the mess.

We followed André out of the barracks and bid Francois, our lookout, adieu. Labeau would arrive at the mess in five minutes, which was just long enough for us to make the underground journey.

"In here," André said as we followed him through the rear entrance to our barracks building. Our barracks shared the same building with classrooms, offices, and even the post barber, but locked doors forbade access to these offices. Entry to the tunnels could be made only by exiting the barracks and re-entering through a door on the far side of the building. André picked the single lock easily. Entering the building, he led us down a flight of stairs to a dead end. "See those boxes?" Ten cardboard boxes stood neatly stacked against the wall at the base of the stairs. "Take'm down."

The boxes were empty, and as we removed them, a four-foot-square hole in the wall made itself known. In single file we climbed through the hole, turned on our flashlights, and followed our Master Ninja to glory and to food.

"Let's see, turn right at this juncture." André was reading from a map that he had made when exploring the tunnels previously. "A short five minutes and we're in." His voice echoed in the tunnel.

Like a trail of fireflies, we advanced through the tunnel until it opened into another hole-in-the-wall.

"We're here," André whispered.

"How can you tell?" Outman asked.

"Smell the grease?" Bryant replied.

"We're here." Don authenticated our arrival.

"Turn off your flashlights. They can be seen through the windows," a voice said.

"Okay, here's the plan." André had obviously rehearsed this momentous quest for food many times in his head. "Outman, you go upstairs to the window and keep an eye on Francois. Let us know if he drops out of his chair." Outman found his way to the stairs and disappeared into the darkness. "Didarksi, find us some bags to carry food. Boxes are okay if you can get them. We'll also need at least five large garbage bags. They're kept in the cupboard over the sink." André had obviously planned this insurrection personally and knew the kitchen well. Officially, it was off limits to recruits. "Teather, you, Lumchuck, Krzyszyk, and Burl follow me."

Within our allotted five minutes we had located and packed six roasted chickens, two flats of cake, four loaves of bread, two pounds of butter, three quarts of milk, and enough plates, knives, forks, and glasses for all the Ninjas.

"One more thing, I almost forgot." André disappeared into a small room. We could hear the clinking of glass and he returned with his own personal cardboard box. "Outman. C'mon, we're outta here," André shout-whispered.

The trail of fireflies departed through the tunnel and returned to the dormitory. Two minutes later Don Outman and Phil Didarski carried Francois up the stairs to the dormitory. The elevator would have been too slow.

"We can't eat this here. Night guards patrol every hour. They'll report us," Lumchuck said, licking his lips. Clearly, it was Christmas and he had temporarily abandoned his plans for losing weight.

"Francois?" André looked in the direction of our friend. "Think we can take them there?"

"Dat would be fine wit me," Francois replied.

Together with our booty and crippled friend, we exited the thirty-two-man dormitory, crossed the hallway, and stopped at a locked door.

"Ever wonder what lies beyond this door?" André asked.

"Nope."

Reaching into his pocket, André retrieved a small piece of stiff spring steel, shaped in a half-circle. Sliding it past the angled throw-bolt, he slid it toward him and the door opened.

"You dirty dog, André," Outman said. "That's from a girl's bra. I thought—"

"It was a going-away present from my Chinese girlfriend," André interrupted. He smiled, then looked sad.

"What's her name?" Krzyszyk asked. "Won Hung Lo?"

We laughed.

"Dat's not funny," Francois said. "Like you, Phil, dis guy lost his girl too." Labeau pointed in André's direction. André's face grew even sadder—like Phil's upon his return from Christmas holiday. Then he looked up and spoke.

"Grab Francois, we got some stairs to climb." It was then that we realized this was the exact location where we had often seen Labeau's wheelchair abandoned. Two flights of stairs, another piece of lock wizardry, and we had arrived at our dining hall. It was a small room measuring approximately ten feet square with an adjoining room off to the right.

"This is the top of the service-elevator shaft," Lumchuck stated.

"Dis is my private gymnasium," Francois whispered, pointing to the iron weights stacked in the corner.

"Give me some light," André commanded, ignoring Larry's comments. A few minutes later a large white tablecloth had been laid on the floor and our feast adorned the centre. André had moved a set of barbells over to the wall. "No workout for you tonight, Labeau," he said, as he reached into his private cardboard box and retrieved a dozen candles. Lighting them, he quietly stated, "Gentlemen, dinner is served."

Plates were passed out and knives and forks were ignored as eight hungry RCMP recruits tore into their chickens like starving carnivores.

"Sshhh!" André placed his finger to his mouth. "Hear that?"

We held our breath, but the air was still, silent.

"Getting a bit spooked, André?" I asked.

"No, I heard something. Never mind, it's gone now."

"What's gone?"

"Footsteps."

Another two minutes passed as we sat in silence, then the quiet was broken by Lumchuck's chewing sounds.

"Why don't we ever get food like this?"

Munch, munch, munch.

"Don't talk wiff your mouf full."

"Munch, munch, munch, swallow."

"André, which cooler did you get this from? We ain't never eaten food like this before."

André ignored the question. Reaching once again into his private booty box he retrieved eight wine glasses and filled them from several tall green bottles.

"André, you're ignoring me." Krzyszyk repeated the question. "Where'd this food come from?"

"The fridge marked O.M.," André replied.

"O.M.?"

"O.M."

"What the flamin' hell does that stand for?"

André passed out the last full wine glass and quietly stated, "Officers' Mess."

"My God, we're going to jail. We're eating an inspector's chicken. That's a commissioned officer's poultry. Oh my God, we're all going to jail." Burl started shaking all over. He was an insecure individual. He prefaced his every comment with "But what will they say?" and the thought of stealing from the Officers' Mess shook him to the core.

Standing at attention, Didarski snapped a salute. "Inspector Chicken. May he rest in peace." We laughed.

"Inspector Chicken, sir!" Don Outman added. "We're safe as long as no one knows," he reassured Harold.

"Officers' Mess," Harold repeated as he sipped his wine, still trembling. "We're eating stolen property."

"Stolen?" André replied. "Stolen? Not on your high brown boots. My fellow troopmates, this is not stolen chicken. It was liberated under the new RCMP initiative titled: Creative Acquisition and Redistribution Program. CARP for short."

"Carp?" Harold repeated.

"Carp."

"We're eating carp?"

"Yes." André smiled. "These fine liberated chickens have merely been acquired and redistributed to the needy. Us."

"Officers' mess—carp." Someone repeated the words, then laughed.

"Gentlemen, a toast." André stood up.

Hoisting Francois to his feet, we held him propped against the wall, and in the candlelight, eight young faces glowed as wine glasses were raised.

"To the Royal Canadian Mounted Police!"

"To the Mountie Makers."

"To Troop 18!"

"To girlfriends—past, present, and future!"

"To freakin' swimming instructors!"

"To harching! To forward harching and to backwards harching!"

"To Didarski's left ear!"

"To Inspector Chicken!"

"To you, Francois, and to the day you can harch with us!"

"To us!"

"To us—best freakin' Ninjas this academy has ever seen!"

"To our Master Ninja!"

"To us!" a voice repeated, and we all drank.

Together we drank, we ate, and we drank again. André had

liberated a total of eight bottles of imported French wine, and we were duty-bound to destroy all evidence.

Between mouthfuls of Inspector Chicken, we all shared stories of our short Christmas holidays. We were not sure if the change was within us or if, indeed, our families had changed, but we all agreed that our lives had taken on a new direction. Then, as the wine bottles emptied, we began to compose and sing our own song.

"Young Mounties, young Mounties, young Mounties are we,
There's no finer Mounties in the RCMP.
A troop of young Mounties so great and so swell,
And we'll graduate from this miserable hell."

One hour later the evidence was carefully wrapped in several plastic trash bags and stowed secretly in the large commercial dumpster located in the small alcove behind our barracks.

That night we slept well, but there was a price to pay for our raid on the Officers' Mess refrigerator. The following morning as we took our seats at the mess hall, we rejected our customary serving of glutinous pancakes and oily bacon in favour of aspirins and powdered milk. Our heads pounded from too much wine, and our stomachs rejected the sticky, greasy disks we had almost grown accustomed to.

For the remaining three months of our training we worried. Had we been caught we would most certainly have been dishonourably discharged. Fired in shame.

But no one ever knew.

Except us.

The Ninjas of Troop 18.

CHAPTER TEN
Physical Education—and Other Such Tortures

Friday, January 5: O–dark something. Morning fatigue parade. We were now four weary months into our six-month imprisonment at Depot. Only two months left—then ... freedom!

"Troop 18, aaatenshuun!" We snapped to attention. "Forward harch!" Marching forward, our troop separated itself from the others as we closed the distance between our ranks and Corporal Withers. "Troop halt!" We stopped.

Corporal Withers spoke in a voice that echoed off the drill hall walls and into every ear. Even Didarski's left ear.

"I have two matters to discuss this morning." Withers walked over to Phil Didarski and spoke—not loud, but in a clear voice we could all hear. "Lost part of a tooth, did we?"

"Yes, Corporal."

Corporal Withers eyed each member of our troop as he spoke. "If I ever hear of this sort of bullshit again in your troop, I'll have you all kicked out. We're on the same side—brothers—no danger, no threat of injury, and no risk of death will ever tear us apart. You are all some bloody useless excuse for Mounties, fighting over a cigar. This troop will be confined to barracks for the next week. There will be no weekend passes and no one will be allowed off base. This type of crap will not be tolerated. Do I make myself perfectly clear?"

"Yes, Corporal," the troop answered.

"I'll be visiting your troop in your dorm. You will have inspections each night, and by all that is holy, your pits had better be the best I have ever seen or you'll never get off base. Once again, do I make myself perfectly clear?"

"Yes, Corporal."

"Look at your senior troop!" he shouted as his finger swung in their direction. "They have pride, spirit, and camaraderie. They have won their scarlet tunics. Keep it up, ladies, and I'll personally see you wearing fatigue jackets for the rest of your lives."

His threat was real and it worried us. Somehow our instructors knew everything that happened. We never understood how they came to learn our troop secrets, but it struck fear into us.

Were secret television cameras planted in our barracks? Could a Corporal become invisible? Were they all psychic? We would never learn their secrets—but they knew ours.

Withers stood back and raised his voice as he continued. "Several freshly roasted chickens have been reported missing from the mess." We stood motionless—except for Harold Burl. He shook visibly. "Would anyone care to offer an explanation?"

Silence.

"Anyone?" he shouted louder.

Silence.

"Good. I wouldn't want to think we were training thieves here at this academy. Cooks probably can't count anyway, so having asked the question, we will set this matter to rest."

Our troop breathed a collective sigh of relief, then smiled as he added, softening his voice, "Maybe some day they'll serve carp at the mess. I heard it's pretty good." Don Withers winked and went on to assign fatigue duties to each troop as the brooms, shovels, brass polish, and toilet brushes were handed out.

"He knows! He bloody well knows," Burl said, still shaking.

"Yeah, and he ain't tellin' nobody," Didarski added as we walked from the parade hall to our awaiting toilets.

"Fine man, that Don Withers." André smiled as he shouldered his toilet brush. "Fine man. He was outside the elevator-room door all the time."

Corporal Withers obviously had been ordered to make enquiries into the missing chickens. Having carried out his assignment as NCO in charge of poultry investigations, he would report that nothing had been learned and the matter would be put to rest.

Fine man.

Two hours later we stood at attention in the gymnasium. Corporal Steel, our physical education instructor, carefully inspected each recruit. Our gym shorts were white, starched, and pressed stiff. Our running shoes gleamed white with several coats of liquid canvas dye, and even the cheap see-through T-shirts we'd been issued were immaculately laundered and pressed for inspection.

Kit inspection, the careful scrutiny of our uniforms, was a daily occurrence. We were inspected at fatigue parade, self-defence class, noon parade, and drill practice, and on occasion we were called out of bed after lights-out for surprise inspections that no one ever quite understood. Toward the end of our training, however, we had reasoned that since all our "after-lights-out" inspections were called by Corporal Thain, our swimming instructor, it probably had more to do with underwear inspection than routine discipline.

After a close inspection, our instructor spoke. "Not bad," he judged us. "Not incredibly good, but not bad."

We were relieved. Any minor speck of dirt on a running shoe, any double crease ironed onto our gym shorts, even a droopy sock, would consign our troop to "ten of the Queen's finest."

The "Queen's finest" was a modified push-up regimen that was both punitive and torturous. Starting from a standing position, we would drop to the floor, execute one push-up, then snap to attention. This would be repeated with two push-ups, followed by three, until the count of ten had been reached. One minor flaw in style would result in the count being restarted at one.

Today would not begin with "ten of the Queen's finest," and we were happy. Today was circuit training, also called Fitness Field Day. Each month we would be tested on a given circuit of exercises, which were brought to the gymnasium straight from hell. As our six-month imprisonment progressed, we would be graded on our individual improvement in such areas as agility, strength, stamina, and ability to refrain from vomiting on the gym floor.

"As you know, fitness is paramount to the success of a police officer."

We had heard this lecture from Corporal Steel many times, but we stood in silent obedience as he once again explained the importance of physical fitness.

In the corner of the room, Francois listened intently. From the frown on his face it seemed as if he was forcing himself to believe every word that Steel spoke.

"We will begin our warming-up exercises prior to the Fitness Field Day tests." A collective groan ushered forth from the troop. "Oh, you don't like warming up? Maybe a few more of the Queen's finest would be better?"

"No, Corporal," thirty-two voices answered.

"Good. We will start with the cradle carry."

During our first class, we had been assigned partners. I drew Lumchuck. He was too fat for me to carry, and although I was the smallest recruit in the troop, Lumchuck could barely hoist me from the ground. "This will make you both improve!" Steel had told us.

"Teather, if you want to survive, you'll make Lumchuck shed some of that fat." He poked Larry's stomach, losing his finger deep into the roll that hung over his shorts. "Lumchuck, if you want to survive as a part of this two-man team, you'll make Teather put some meat on those skinny, pathetic bones of his." The symbiotic relationship had worked well. In four months I had gained strength; Larry only had another twenty pounds to shed.

Jumping into Lumchuck's outstretched arms, I could feel his fat chest jiggle as he carried me the length of the gym. It was an awkward feeling, being carried against Larry's chest. He had breasts that would put most of Regina's young women to shame. Once we arrived at the opposite end, we reversed roles and I carried him back. Compared to when I had arrived in Hades, my legs were stronger, and since my cargo also had become lighter, at this halfway point in our training we were no longer the slowest in the troop.

After twenty minutes of cradle carries, chin-ups, and other small tortures, we were ready to begin our Fitness Field Day.

"This should sweat that turkey out of your bodies," Steel said. "You did have Christmas turkey, didn't you, Lumchuck?"

"No, Corporal. I ate chicken."

We smiled.

"Well, you ate too much," Steel replied.

We took turns completing the series of exercises while a watchful instructor armed with a stopwatch recorded our time. The test was an agonizing ten minutes long. One-third of the troop watched, one-third replaced cones and hurdles that had been knocked over, and one-third ran the gauntlet of obstacles and climbing ropes.

We jumped hurdles, lifted weights, executed chin-ups on an overhead bar, and lifted more weights. Each torturous cycle left us all gasping for air and weak with exhaustion. Failure to improve on last month's score meant extra gym classes in the evening, and no one relished that punishment. Under the watchful evil-eye of Corporal Steel, evening gym classes were agonizing, abusive, and painful. Lumchuck was made to wear a sweatsuit covered with a plastic garbage bag in order to "sweat them calories away." Unfortunately, heat exhaustion resulted in Larry losing weight from vomiting, not from "sweating them calories away."

Injuries were common during these evening tortures from hell. Muscles were torn, ligaments stretched, and spines compressed. It was Corporal Steel's favourite time. But not ours.

We completed our Fitness Field Day exercises and stood, each of us cloaked in fear and sweat, anxiously awaiting the results.

"Not bad." Corporal Steel sounded like a broken record. "Not incredibly good, but not bad." Steel glanced across the gymnasium. We followed his line of sight. Out of the corner of our eyes, we saw Francois repeatedly raise a steel barbell over his head.

"That's 125 pounds, lads. Looks to me like a cripple could show you all a lesson or two."

One hundred and twenty-five pounds! I still had not reached the minimum required weight that Francois was hoisting repeatedly. In order to graduate, each recruit had to be able to raise, at least once, the weight that Francois was toying with.

"Not bad. Not incredibly good, but not bad," Corporal Steel repeated.

Francois was sweating.

André was smiling. His student was doing well.

"And now, since you lads have done so well on your Fitness Field Day, I have a special treat in store for you."

We listened to Steel, hoping against all odds that we would not be disappointed. We were.

"I think a nice run in the cool prairie air would perk us all up. Wouldn't it?"

"Yes, Corporal," we obediently agreed. We knew that if one more troop groan was given in response, his revenge would have been brutal and swift.

The weather had abated. The outside temperature was above freezing, and it felt only cool as we went out the rear door of the gymnasium. Our run took us three miles along a country gravel road before we returned to base. Corporal Steel set a merciless pace, and we followed, fearing punishment every step of the way should we not keep up with our instructor.

One mile into the run he mocked us by turning around and running backwards. Keeping cadence with our step, he sang:

"I don't know what I believe,
I've been home for Christmas Eve.
I'm so young and I'm so fat,
The RCMP is where it's at.
Running's fun and we're not slow,
And we all love this freakin' snow."

As we sang along, the words were ingrained deep into our hearts, minds, and souls. The first line cleared our brains of useless thoughts. The second gave us hope that some day we might return home again. The rest of the song ate at any egos we had left, and the endless repetition hypnotized our conscious minds into believing that our cross-country run was actually enjoyable.

It was a painful lesson—but a necessary one if we were to survive as police officers. The border between pain and pleasure, between fear and accomplishment, was again being crossed.

"We will teach you to discover your personal limits—then go beyond them. Having surpassed your personal limitations, you will then be afforded a totally new outlook on life." Corporal Steel's first lecture to us during our first lesson was indelibly stamped on my brain. "When you lads graduate from this academy, you will have no limits. Nothing will ever hold you back. Limits are what you set on yourself!" he shouted. "I will not allow you to set limits in my gymnasium. I will not set limits to your performance and I will not allow you to limit yourselves. If I ever detect any of you reaching your own personal limit, I'll kick your arse to a new and higher level of performance."

Then he added in a softer voice, "Lads, for the rest of your lives, you will encounter countless people trying to limit your abilities. It doesn't make sense to help them."

Corporal Steel was a persuasive man. After our first day in the gym, no one acknowledged the words "can't," "impossible," or "limits." With his goading persistence we became invincible. That simple fact was irrefutable. Our instructor told us so.

Later that day, after we had recovered from our prairie-winter run, we dined on mystery meat and rubber carrots.

"How do they do this?" Burl asked. "How in the name of all that is good to eat can they rubberize a carrot?"

"The same way they disguise the meat," someone offered.

"Who knows, we could be eating recycled recruits," a voice whispered.

"The potatoes are horrible," another voice added.

"They're not potatoes," said a voice f rom across the table. "They're turnips. Albino turnips. Used to feed them to the hogs." Don Outman, our resident prairie dog, shook his head from side to side. "Ain't no one should be made to eat this."

With as little chewing as possible, we swallowed—most of it. Don and a few others left their albino turnips uneaten, but most of us were able to flip the food over our tongues and gulp hard.

Dessert, this night, was palatable. Imprisoned in a small bowl sat red jello with small unknown objects suspended inside. As we cut through the wiggly mass, we took turns trying to identify what lay incarcerated within.

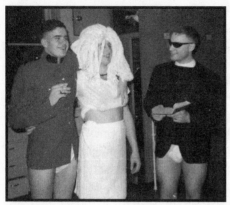

FORGIVENESS

Troop 18, January 1968. After a fight, the combatants were often encouraged to undergo an official "marriage ceremony" to demonstrate their forgiveness, and reaffirm their troop vows. "Ninjas All!"

"Marshmallows."

"Pink marshmallows."

"Baby mice."

"Pink baby mice."

"I got a blue one."

"Very cold baby mice."

"Old meat."

"New cheese."

"Fumunda cheese," Outman suggested.

"Fumunda cheese?" a voice asked. "Where do you get fumunda cheese?"

"Fumunda your armpits."

Spontaneous laughter erupted. Forbidden laughter. We were safe. No NCOs had shared supper with us this evening, so laughter had won the moment.

"Fumunda your armpits." Lumchuck repeated the words, laughing so hard that tiny projectiles of jello flew from his nose.

"Fumunda your nose, Lumchuck," Outman added.

Fumunda cheese and baby mice jello joined shepherd's pie, slippery bacon, and pancakes as new additions to the menu from hell.

One hour later we sat in our dormitory, shining shoes and preparing for the first of seven evening inspections. Each recruit sat on the floor, cross-legged, applying coats of shoe polish to his boots with a moistened cloth.

"I tink I got it easy," Francois said. "Since I don't walk much, my shoes aren't scuffed."

"Yeah," Burl replied. "I wish I was you."

"Bite your tongue, lad," Didarski shouted. For one recruit to call another "lad" was the supreme insult.

"Phys ed sure was tough today, eh?"

"Yeah, but not as tough as this inspection's gonna be."

"C'mon, guys, we only have an hour. The floors have to be waxed yet and our walls dusted."

"Aw, man, who spilled the bottle of aftershave lotion in the can?" Burl had just returned from the washroom.

"I did dat," Francois replied. "Sorry."

"Man, if Withers gets a smell of that, we're toast."

Corporal Withers conducted our inspections. He was a fair man, and no one really understood why he seemed to have turned against us. His discipline had become unfriendly and brutal.

"Don't worry, he won't go in de can—not after Lumchuck gets trew in dere," Francois replied.

Within an hour, we stood at attention by our beds and awaiting the appearance of Corporal Withers. At 2000 hours—precisely—the clock over the entrance doors heralded his arrival. The red second hand attained a vertical position and the double doors swung open. Corporal Withers was on time. To the very second.

Slowly, he walked down the centre of the dormitory. On each side, pits had cloned themselves and appeared identical, save for the name card posted on the wall above each bed.

Withers was silent, as were we. He surveyed each member of the troop. Our clothes were pressed immaculately. We had long ago learned to iron the sheets after our beds were made. No creases showed this night.

"If I find as much as one speck of dust in here, I'll add a day to your punishment." Withers spoke firmly. Wiping his forefinger over the window sills, he studied it, then frowned. "So far, so good."

We knew that Corporal Withers' inspection would be thorough—thorough, but fair. After all, he had held secret our Ninja raid and the carped chickens.

Corporal Withers' leather riding crop was a testament to the days when recruits trained for nine months, instead of six. Traditionally, three months were devoted to equestrian training. We had missed the last of these historic trimesters by one year. The mere possession of a leather riding crop commanded the respect and awe of all recruits.

Corporal Withers raised his leather crop over his head and drew it down hard onto Ken Krzyszk's wool blanket. A cloud of lint rose in the air.

"That's one," Withers said.

Francois sat in his wheelchair at the foot of his bed—erect. Dragging the sole of his high brown boots over Francois' mirror shine, Withers spoke. "What did you shine your shoes with, lad? Peanut butter and steel wool?" Francois did not answer. "That's two."

Leaning over to check the alignment of the beds, Withers again found fault. "Didarski, your bed doesn't line up with the others. That's three!" he shouted.

We had checked our bed alignment immediately prior to the inspection. They were perfectly aligned. Withers was finding fault where none existed.

"I see that you all like being confined to barracks. Let's make it eight days, lads. Shall we?"

"Yes, Corporal."

"Oh, I almost forgot—your lavatory smells like a cheap whore-house." Withers turned in my direction. "Doesn't it, Teather?"

"I don't know, Corporal."

"What do you mean, you don't know?"

"I've never been in a CHEAP whorehouse, Corporal."

Withers smiled. It was an involuntary reflex. "You like being funny, Teather?" he said.

"Yes, Corporal."

"Good. You can hand in one hundred jokes, neatly typed, on my desk by Monday morning. No typing errors, no strike-overs and no erasures. Do I make myself clear?"

"Yes, Corporal."

"And they had better be good ones."

"Yes, Corporal.

"I think we have a problem here, with discipline. Don't we, Teather?"

Knowing I had nothing to lose, I replied, "What do you mean, WE, Corporal? You got tapeworms?"

"Make that two hundred jokes."

"Yes, Corporal."

I had everything to lose.

"Goodnight lads. See you all tomorrow night." He turned and left through the same doors he had entered.

Francois stared at the scuffed toe-cap of his right shoe. Phil knelt down, eyeing the alignment of his bed with the others. "It's perfect," he said. "Sonofabitch. It's perfect."

We took turns hitting our wool blankets and watching in dismay as a cloud of lint rose into the air. To remove all lint would be an impossible task.

"We'll never get out of here," Burl said. "We're prisoners."

The speaker played "lights out," and thirty-two men crawled into their beds.

"G'night guys," Phil called out.

"G'night Phil," we all answered.

All except Burl, who sobbed, "We'll never get out of here."

> "Make your decision based on what is ethical ... not on what you fear will bring punishment or praise, but what you deem to be noble and just."
>
> Corporal Don Withers

CHAPTER ELEVEN
Driver Training—Death Spins and Wheat Fields

Monday, January 8: We had endured a weekend of "stand-to" inspections, but Corporal Withers had managed to find fault with our barracks housekeeping on both Saturday and Sunday evenings. As was predictable, some of his critique was valid but some was not. This had bothered us more and more.

Why had this instructor we had come to admire turned against us? Why was he duty-bound to destroy our morale? Why did he no longer treat us fairly and with respect?

Why had we not been able to eliminate our lint?

We pondered these questions silently, standing at attention in the post garage. The post garage was located a short walk from our barracks. Security of the vehicles was of paramount importance, and the placing of the garage close to the barracks ensured a degree of security.

It was our first day of instruction in Advanced Driver Training. Before "advanced" had entered our vocabulary, we had driven the streets of Regina and the country roads, obeying all rules of the road, all speed limits, and all directions given to us by our driving instructor.

Today would be different. Much different.

"Good morning, girls," Corporal William Hall called out as he entered the garage.

"Good morning, Corporal," we answered, smiling as we responded. Driver Training was unique among classes. That had been made clear during our first lesson.

"Listen up, girls," Corporal Hall had said as he smiled at us. "Driver Training is different than all the other classes you will take here. You will be making decisions—life and death decisions— behind the wheel of a police vehicle. This isn't theory, and from your first basic lesson through to your most advanced driving manoeuvres,

I want your hearts, souls, brains, hands, and feet totally involved with the vehicle. We will be informal during all my lessons." He paused for a moment, smiled, then added, "You will call me 'Corporal' and I will call you 'girls.'"

"Girls?" Lumchuck repeated.

"That's right, Miss. Girls."

We had laughed, visualizing Lumchuck in a skirt. It was not a pretty sight.

We had heard many rumours about the lessons in advanced driving techniques. This facet of our training would be dangerous, we knew that, but we were ready.

Or so we thought.

"You have probably heard that we average one serious car accident each month during this phase of training," Corporal Hall addressed our troop. "Well, that's wrong. We average two per month and injuries are commonplace. As you know, last week a member of Troop 17 rolled his car and sent all four occupants to the hospital." He rubbed his left elbow. "I was lucky—got out with only a sprained elbow. Constable Parson, however, will have a nice train track left on his face after they remove the stitches." He smiled. "Do you still want to go out today and play, girls?"

"Yes, Corporal."

We were eager to drive faster, harder, and wilder than any recruit had ever driven before.

"Okay, Lumchuck, Bryant, Teather, and Outman—you're with me. The rest of you wait here for the other driving instructors."

Together we climbed into the marked car as Corporal Hall drove from the garage. "Good luck, ladies!" he called out loudly as we turned and left the base.

"Let's put a few miles on this beast to warm up the engine and brakes." Our police car was hardly a beast. Perhaps "tired old basset hound" would have been a more fitting descriptive. Because of the high accident rate, the cars we drove were those that had been condemned by various detachments. While they awaited their final disposal to Crown Assets, we were allowed to drive them. Brakes squealed, exhaust pipes belched smoke, and the manual steering wiggled as we travelled down the road. These were hardly beasts, but the oversized engines gave us what we wanted: speed.

Our eyes grew wide as our instructor accelerated to eighty miles per hour, then ninety. Once we reached and maintained a speed of one hundred miles per hour, he spoke. "Sort of purrs along, doesn't she?"

We were silent.

"Newton's First Law of Motion, ladies, is: An object will continue to move in a straight line or remain at rest unless acted upon by an external force." Then he added, "We are now northbound." As he spoke the words, he slammed on the brakes, and all four wheels locked tight. Hall turned the steering wheel sharply, but the vehicle continued its straight-line trajectory.

"When your wheels are locked, you have no steering," he pointed out. Quickly he decelerated to fifty miles per hour. He removed his foot from the brake and the car snapped 180 degrees. "We are now southbound," he confidently stated, and once again accelerated to one hundred miles per hour.

"That is called a gravel-road turn. Anyone care to try it?"

Don Outman was first behind the wheel. His gravel-road turn was impeccable, and it impressed Corporal Hall.

"Where'd you learn to drive like that?" Hall asked.

"Works better with a case of open beer in the trunk, Corporal," Don replied. Don had grown up on the prairies, and it was obvious he had gained experience escaping from patrolling police officers as he and his friends drove the country roads in search of girls, good times, and happy memories.

"Case of beer in the trunk?" Hall repeated.

"Just kidding, Corporal. I was always the designated driver. They never let me drink. My buddies always said that my driving was too crazy when I was sober. No one wanted to be in the car if I'd been drinking."

"I can see why. Did you ever get caught?"

"No, Corporal."

"Let's see you do that again."

Outman gave another demonstration of his prairie driving skills, then added two variations. The first adaptation he called the "wheels in the ditch" turn.

As the right side of the car began to slide past the gravel shoulder and into the ditch, Don cranked the wheel hard left. In less than a second, the vehicle spun around and headed off in the opposite direction.

The second manoeuvre was aptly titled "the death spin." The death spin was a 360-degree spin that ended with the vehicle resuming its original heading. "That's just to confuse them into thinking I'm gonna run in the opposite direction," Prairie Dog smiled.

"Okay, I've had enough." Corporal Hall directed the car to the side of the road.

"I really like that Newton Law of Motion stuff," Outman said. "He must have been some driver."

We stood beside the car, breathing in the cold air. Lumchuck had turned a deeper-than-normal shade of blue and stood poised and ready to drop his bacon and pancakes onto the shoulder of the road.

"Puke in my car and you're walking home," Hall said.

Lumchuck let fly.

"There, that'll help you lose some weight, Larry," André said as Lumchuck bent over, gagged, and spewed more pancakes.

"That's disgusting," Corporal Hall said. "Lumchuck, you're an environmental hazard. Did you know that?"

"Yes, Corporal."

"Here, have a mint, puke-breath. You're next behind the wheel."

"Yes, Corporal."

Lumchuck soon took us all to the brink of death. Like Prairie Dog, Larry had invented his own version of a high-speed gravel-road turn.

"Lumchuck," Hall said, "you really have gone where no man has gone before, haven't you?"

"Yes, Corporal."

At one hundred miles per hour Corporal Hall's eyes grew wide. Above the rattle of the engine, our instructor spoke to Larry. "Have you read any books by Doctor Raymond Moody or Elizabeth Kubler-Ross?"

"About life after death?" Lumchuck asked.

"Yes."

"I certainly have."

"How about you, Teather, and you other ladies in the back seat? Ever read those books about life after death? About the experience of travelling down a long tunnel toward a light—meeting loved ones who have passed away?"

"Yes, Corporal." They were best-sellers, and we had read books by both authors.

As we spoke, Lumchuck locked up the brakes, slid onto the gravel shoulder, and spun the steering wheel. "Head for the light at the end of the tunnel!" Hall screamed. "Head for the light!"

We all laughed as Lumchuck's car careened out of control, spinning its way to a full stop approximately twenty feet from the road.

"Parking in a wheat field, ladies, is an offence. I'll have to cite you for this, Lumchuck."

Larry blushed.

"One thing, Corporal?" Don Outman spoke from the rear seat. "This Newton guy—the one that makes the laws about movement and such?"

"Yes."

"Well, he was wrong about something remaining at rest or continuing to move in a straight line unless acted upon by an external force."

"Wrong?"

"Yes, wrong. Lumchuck is clearly an internal force, and we haven't moved in a straight line since he took the wheel."

"You're right, Outman." Hall looked at Larry, still shaking from his latest manoeuvre.

"You're right. Lumchuck, take your place in the rear seat. It's André's turn."

As André Bryant took his place behind the wheel, he displayed his usual state of cool, courage, and confidence.

"I've heard about you, Bryant," Hall said.

"Oh."

"Yeah, something about you being some kind of Ninja or something?"

No one answered.

"Well, let's see if you can Ninja your way out of this lesson. I want you to duplicate Outman's moves. I want you to duplicate each turn, including the death spin—and I want you to improve on it."

Corporal Hall had given André an impossible task. Don Outman was clearly a better driver than our instructor, and the possibility of André Bryant improving on his manoeuvres seemed impossible.

For a minute, André sat behind the wheel and stared through the front windshield of the parked police vehicle. He revved the engine a couple of times, and the torque from the motor rocked the car.

"Put it in gear, the fan won't pull it," Hall directed.

Reaching out, André slammed the car into gear, and we accelerated along the shoulder and onto the road. As we again approached one hundred miles per hour, André spoke in a forced Scottish accent. "We're at warp nine, Captain. The dilithium crystals just can't take any more. Our anti-gravity containment field is about to collapse. She's a good ship, captain, but she just can't take any more." Then switching to an excellent imitation of Captain Kirk of the Starship *Enterprise*, he answered himself. "Scotty, I don't want excuses, I want speed. If the Romulans are capable of warp ten, so are we."

The police car accelerated beyond our maximum allowed speed.

"Slow 'er down," Hall said. He was serious.

"Can't, Captain. I've got my orders," replied the Scottish voice. "I have to improve on Outman's performance. She's a good ship, she'll take it."

"Mother of God," Hall said. "He's gonna kill us all."

In an instant, Bryant locked the brakes, spun the steering wheel, and executed a 360-degree turn while tuning in his favourite radio station. Then he turned to Corporal Hall and spoke. "Captain, I think we've lost the Romulans. Request permission to drop out of warp."

"Permission granted, Scotty. Drop out of warp and park this thing or I'll kick you outta Starfleet."

My move to the driver's seat proved anticlimactic. I would not even attempt to match the driving skills of André or Don. Nor would I park in a wheat field. However, my conservative driving skills seemed to please Corporal Hall. He had survived enough death spins for one morning.

One hour later, we pulled into the post garage, rolled out the hoses, washed our beast, and parked it in its designated stall.

Other troopmates returned with their driving instructors, and we all washed the vehicles while the instructors compared notes in the corner of the garage. We watched Corporal Hall hold an imaginary steering wheel and spin in a circle. We watched as the other instructors began to laugh. Two of them had already experienced the driving skills of Don Outman and André Byrant.

With all cars parked, we lined up against the wall in troop formation. Approaching our troop, the instructors checked their notes, looked at each other, and smiled.

"Okay, ladies, we have a verbal test for you to complete." Corporal Hall was smiling. He enjoyed our light-hearted humour and wanted to demonstrate to the other instructors the rapport he had with our troop. "We have prepared a series of questions. This will be a verbal test. You will be given no time to formulate an answer. Driving demands instant thinking and immediate reaction. Failure to answer instantly will result in another day being added to your barracks confinement and another evening inspection. Do I make myself perfectly clear?"

"Yes, Corporal."

"Didarski, do you yield for a blind pedestrian at a crosswalk?"

"No need to, Corporal. He can't see my licence number."

"You're a sick lady, Didarski."

"Yes, Corporal."

"Teather, what is the difference between a flashing red light and a flashing amber light?"

"The colour."

"Outman, who has the right-of-way when four cars approach an uncontrolled intersection simultaneously?"

"The pickup truck with the rear-window gun rack and the bumper sticker that says: 'Guns don't kill people, I do!'"

"Bryant, what are some points to remember when passing a vehicle?"

"Wave if she's good-looking. Don't let them see your coffee cup. Hold your car's radio microphone to your lips so they think you have an urgent call instead of an appointment at the doughnut shop."

"Lumchuck, what is your primary consideration when parking your police car?"

"Don't have one, Corporal," Larry replied, pointing to the RCMP crest on the police car and the proud image of a buffalo. "Buffalo cabs can park wherever they like."

"Burl, when driving through thick fog, what should you use?"

"Your car."

Some quips were better than others. The banter continued for another five minutes with Corporal Hall furiously making notes. As the session ended, he tore the pages from his pad and handed them to me.

"Seems like you'll be asked for more jokes, Teather. That is your usual punishment, isn't it? Typing jokes?" Hall had obviously spoken to our other instructors. "Before your troop graduates, you'll likely lose many more weekend passes and spend most of your time in the typing hall, hammering out jokes. Here, take these. As lame as they are, they may help."

"Thanks, Corporal."

"Ladies, today has been no small moment in my life. I truly have been taken where no man has gone before and I offer a special thanks to Lumchuck, whose parking abilities will not go unremembered." Then his face grew serious, and he paused for a moment before he spoke. "All this joking, all the snappy comebacks, all the answers you have given, show me you are learning to think on your feet. From this day forth, I want you all to carry one lesson with you."

We stood silently. Corporal Hall had lost his smile.

"When you graduate, you will be required to chase cars, to catch the bad guys, to respond code three—red lights and siren—and you will be required to drive fast. Too fast at times. You will have no choice, so remember this." He drew a deep breath and continued, "You will be required to make decisions in a fraction of a second. After you make your split-second decision, your superiors and yes, even the courts, will spend months and years deciding if your decision was just, reasonable, and valid. In this class you must learn to think quick, execute your decisions, and then be prepared to stand behind them."

Hall took three paces backwards, and in a rather uncharacteristic, formal move, he snapped to attention and shouted, "Troop 18, dismissed!"

As we left the post garage, we could hear the laughter of our driving instructors.

It had been a good lesson. We enjoyed driving class and we appreciated the informality of the instructors. Driving was a disciplined subject and it was stressful, but the instructors' casual, sometimes spontaneous approach allowed us to learn quickly not only to drive, but also to think, react, and make fast decisions.

Lunch came and went at the Road Kill Cafe and we survived the afternoon with only minor injuries. During small-arms training, Lumchuck received a sliver of lead in his hand from an ill-fitting chamber on his revolver, Outman suffered a swollen ear as a result of a fall during self-defence training, and Francois bruised both knees when his barbell slipped during physical training. Didarski suffered the most inventive injury when, just after dining at the mess, he slipped on a patch of bacon grease and hit his head on a chair.

It was a routine day.

Needles was kept busy.

That evening we sat in our barracks and polished shoes, told tall tales of our driver training class, and prepared for another inspection by our turncoat acquaintance, Corporal Don Withers.

"Anyone hazard a guess why he's turned on us?" a voice called out.

"Screw you. Just keep shining them freakin' boots or we'll never get out of here."

BARRACKS INSPECTION

(Troop 18, February 1968) Kit was polished and set out on the bed in "regimental fashion" for nightly barracks inspection. The placement of each article of clothing was often measured. Individuality was not allowed.

"Screw you too!" another voice added. We had become a bitter troop. Profanity and insults were hurled without motive or reason.

Tension was mounting, and it surfaced inside the troop as an insidious, scheming, treacherous monster that was beginning to turn us against each other. The stress and tension we experienced had become a cancer that was eating us from within. We had earned a reputation as the "troop from hell." Friendships were tried and tempers flared, yet in the midst of our own internal warfare, small islands of compassion and camaraderie surfaced.

We had two hours to prepare for our evening inspection. The dormitory smelled like shoe polish, brass cleaner, and floor wax.

"Didarski, watch my gun for me, will ya? I gotta hit the can," Outman called out to Phil. They had been sitting together, polishing their ankle boots, trading stories, and sharing cigars.

"Sure," Phil answered. "But be quick eh?"

We were never allowed to leave our sidearms unattended. Don, however, had just washed his white lanyard, and although it would dry quickly, a weight was needed to stop it from curling. A clean lanyard encircling the neck and ending at the butt of each revolver always pleased Corporal Withers.

Phil watched as Don left the dormitory; then, after a quick glance at his friend's gun, he continued to apply polish to his boots with a moist rag.

Two minutes later the door flew open.

Jumping to attention, we stood motionless, looking at Corporal Withers. He was two hours early.

"At ease, lads," he said, "just passing through." Our dormitory was equipped with double doors at each end. Instructors often used "passing through" as an excuse to drop in unannounced.

Withers walked down the corridor between the beds, stopped, and turned. Looking at Phil Didarski, his eyes scanned the lone revolver, still hanging from its lanyard.

"Nice clean lanyard, lad."

"Thank you, Corporal."

"Is that your gun?"

Phil's face grew red. He was faced with a decision to either lie and risk being caught, or inform on his friend—the one who had broken his tooth five days earlier.

He had to make a decision and make one quick. "It's mine, Corporal."

We heard the response and held our breath. Not a sound, not a whisper, could be heard. We all knew that Phil was lying. We also knew that lying was an offence that would not be tolerated. Lying always meant severe punishment, often recommendation for immediate discharge from the Force.

"Yours, eh?" Withers confirmed.

"Yes, Corporal."

Corporal Withers was not stupid. He walked over, took the revolver in his hand, and held the butt to his eyes.

"What is the serial number?" he asked. From the first day at the academy, we had been counselled to memorize the serial numbers of our revolvers, and we had been quizzed on this many times during our training.

"Corporal?" Phil asked, stalling for time.

"You heard me, lad. What serial number am I looking at?"

"I don't know, Corporal."

"You don't know your own serial number?"

"Forgot it, Corporal."

"Okay. I will add one week's barracks confinement to your punishment. You will remain confined to barracks for a period of seven days after your troop is released. Is that clear?"

"Yes, Corporal."

"Oh, and by the way … " Corporal Withers spoke softly as he leaned toward Didarski, "Nice move, bucko. If you had squealed on your partner I'd have seen you confined to barracks for the rest of your training."

Phil took a deep breath. "Yes, Corporal."

Looking around the room, Withers spoke briefly.

"About time. You can all learn something from this man." Then he added, "Get that tooth fixed, Didarski, you look like a fool when you smile."

"Yes, Corporal!" Phil called out loudly as he smiled and watched Don Withers march out of the dorm.

"What was that all about?" Outman asked, returning from the washroom.

"Nothing," Phil answered. "Nothing, Prairie Dog. Nothing at all."

We sat quietly, contemplating Didarski's bravery. He had risked suspension to cover for his friend, and Withers had not only forgiven this transgression, he had endorsed it. Was that what this was all about? Loyalty? To each other? Was this the ultimate lesson Corporal Withers wanted us to learn? We gathered around Phil's pit, shook his hand, and congratulated him.

A lack of commitment to each other. That was why we were confined to barracks. Dust had nothing to do with the reason for our punishment.

Don Withers had become our enemy. We could only defeat him if we united.

"All for one?" André said.

"One for all!" someone shouted.

"Troop 18 rules!" another voice roared.

"And dat is dat!" Francois added.

We failed our inspection that night. Imaginary dust had once again beaten us.

We had failed again. But we failed together. As an individual troop. Troop 18.

Ninjas all!

"The person by far the most likely to kill you is yourself."
Corporal Daryl Quigley

CHAPTER TWELVE
Small Arms—and Big Lessons

Tuesday, January 30: Three more weeks passed by and only two months remained to graduation. Our troop had vanquished the invisible dust monster and our stand-to inspections were complete. Freedom was once again ours, and we revelled in our success as we whisper-talked over lunch.

"I'll never put vinegar on french fries again," Outman declared. The successful tactic we had used to overcome Corporal Withers' stern discipline was a simple ploy, but one that had worked.

It was a dastardly deed of espionage.

Watching us condemned under the scrutiny of Don Withers, the senior troops refused to help. They had been through similar punishment and forced to find their own solutions. We were abandoned like lepers to suffer and seek our own relief.

It was a penance many troops went through. We later learned that any instructor who felt a troop was not evolving from "a troop of individuals to an individual troop" levied this punishment. The instructors planned a series of stand-to inspections that were impossible for any troop to pass unless they united. To survive, individuals had to forgo their petty differences. The instructor became a formidable foe uncontested by a troop of individuals. He could be vanquished only by the ultimate force—an individual troop.

To defeat our avenging Corporal, we had slowly consolidated our limited talents and wisdom. We were learning that an individual troop could survive and overcome any hardship.

The dust that Corporal Withers raised from our wool blankets each time he hit the covers with his riding crop was not imaginary. It was pervasive. We had dry-cleaned our blankets and beaten them in the cold, dry air. In desperation we had even patted them down with countless rolls of sticky tape. Still, dust rose to the occasion each time Withers whaled his leather crop.

André Bryant, our master Ninja, discovered a solution. He assigned us, in groups of five, to walk nonchalantly through other dormitories the evening before Thursday-morning inspection. We were to pretend we were merely passing through on our way to some obscure destination, and we should neither loiter nor talk with the members of the senior troops.

"The senior troops have the same blankets as we do," André deduced. "It is up to us to discover their solution. Gentlemen, we must resort to spying, and Francois ... " Francois' eyes perked up as he was called, " ... you will be our point man. They won't suspect you; just work on their sympathy. You're a legend here."

"I can do dat," Francois smiled.

After our mission, we reported back to our dormitory.

André was waiting. "Well, gentlemen, what did you see?

No one had an answer. No one had been able to discover any solutions to the wool-blanket dust monster.

"I am sorry, André." Francois looked sad. "I tried everyting I could do and I saw nutting. I looked everywhere but de only ting dey had dat we didn't was spray bottles."

"Spray bottles?"

"Dey were in der washroom. A whole cabinet of spray bottles."

"What was in them?" André asked.

"Dey were just full of water. No cleaner, just water."

"That's it!" André shouted. "That's it! They spray their blankets moments before inspection. A moist surface won't give off dust."

"Yes!" someone cheered.

"But there's one thing we must do to repay our senior troops for their kindness in sharing this secret." André's fertile mind was racing. His ever-widening smile told us he had a plan.

"Kindness? Dey didn't tell us anyting," Francois said.

"That's right, my friend, and that's why we must repay them."

André formulated another plan. Late that night a small brigade of Ninjas made their way through the dusty tunnels and once again raided the Mess. When we returned with a box of spray bottles and two gallons of vinegar, André's plan took shape.

Shortly after midnight, we skulked our way into the washrooms of the senior troops and silently replaced their water spray bottles with ones laced with vinegar.

We planned to have the cleanest and the most unpolluted barracks on base. All others would smell of vinegar.

André was not finished. He was crafting Troop 18's coming-out statement, and while vinegar was the opening paragraph, he insisted on a strong conclusion.

Under the cover of darkness we would run through each dormitory and upset beds while screaming at the tops of our lungs, "Troop 19 rules the world!" Troop 19, our junior troop by two weeks, had developed an attitude. Cockiness and conceit toward senior troops had not earned them any popularity points. In fact, they were despised and shunned; they fought with other troops and amongst themselves. Calling out their name during our raid would ensure broad revenge.

Troop 19 was about to experience an attitude adjustment.

After declaring the victory raid of Troop 19 and wreaking havoc, we made a hasty escape through the tunnels to our barracks block. We left the rest of the base in shambles and listened intently as each troop took revenge on Troop 19. Stunned and confused, Troop 19 retaliated. All dormitories suffered escalating damage.

Troop 18 would be immune to any indiscriminate retaliation, however. Using broom handles and wire, we secured the doors to our dormitory, thus making entry impossible.

The plan had been executed. The following morning at fatigue parade, all troops were confined to barracks for one full week.

All troops except ours.

We had broken with the discipline taught at the academy. No one knew if it was just a release from the stress of training or if a contagious mental disease had pervaded our troop, but it was fun.

Approaching our troop, Corporal Withers asked calmly, "And you lads had nothing to do with any of this, did you?"

"No, Corporal."

Withers said nothing but his eyes spoke volumes. He knew.

It felt good.

Our inspection Thursday morning was the crowning glory. A small amount of moisture sprayed on the blankets, and we passed. The barracks raids left our seniors so confused that their replaced water spray bottles had gone unnoticed. Vinegar spray, in liberal amounts, added another week to their barracks confinement.

Troop 18 ruled Regina!

Somehow the mystery meat served for lunch at the mess became palatable. The sour taste of the meat was garnished with the taste of victory. In the next three weeks we passed all stand-to inspections. We had won the respect of our instructors—including Corporal Don Withers. Although they never openly discussed or even acknowledged our tactics, their smiles and change of attitude toward us told us everything we needed to know.

We had won! As an individual troop.

Lunch became an ugly memory as we dressed for noon parade. Because of our troop's progress, we were now issued with high brown boots, scarlet tunics, and Stetsons.

"You have earned your spurs," Corporal Wheeler had announced during drill class. "As a troop, you will now appear suitably attired for noon parade. Not bad, lads. Not incredibly good, but not bad," he added, borrowing the expression from our phys ed instructor.

We knew better. We had become incredibly good.

Quickly returning to barracks after noon parade, we changed into our working uniform of khaki fatigues, strapped on our sidearms, and prepared for our next class: Small Arms Training.

We stood against the rear wall of the indoor range as Corporal Quigley, our Small Arms instructor, addressed us.

Quigley was not a big man vertically, but his width made up for his lack of height. Possessed of a build similar to Lumchuck's, he would proudly proclaim, "The only difference between you and me, Lumchuck, is that I'm made of muscle and you're fat."

Corporal Daryl Quigley was thirty-four years old and had spent most of his career working highway patrol. No one knew how he had become a Small Arms instructor, but that did not matter. He was the best. The fact that Quigley's lessons were usually short was a relief. His voice was akin to fingernails clawing a chalkboard. In moments of excitement his voice rose to a frequency that only stray dogs could hear. Fortunately, he was a man of few words. Long sentences made us nauseous.

"Concentration, lads." He spoke to our troop. "Concentration and focus." Turning to face his target, Corporal Quigley drew his .38 calibre revolver in one smooth move and pointed it toward the silhouette at the far end of the range. In a matter of less than a second, his faced glazed over like a honey doughnut and we were shut out of his world. His entire universe held only three items— himself, his revolver, and the paper target.

In rapid sequence he emptied his gun. Five shots, a brief pause, and a sixth. Holstering his sidearm, he reached down and cranked a wheel that retrieved his target along a steel cable. He ripped the target from its holder and held it up for all to see.

Five bullet holes were clustered in an area less than four inches wide, in the centre of the silhouette's chest. A sixth shot had punched a hole in the target's left eye.

"Just for good measure," he said as he poked his finger through the eye hole and wiggled it at us.

"Anyone can shoot a paper target. Even you, Lumchuck. What I cannot teach you in this class is how to react to a real threat." Looking around the room, he added, "Anyone in this troop ever been shot at?"

There was no answer.

"Well, I have." Corporal Quigley's eyes looked down to the floor. His limp was almost imperceptible. Only Francois had noticed it.

"How you will behave when looking down the barrel of a hostile gun is a discovery you will not make here. I hope few of you will ever face that problem, but if you do, I want you to remember today's lesson."

Then, in his caustic voice, he continued. "What is your first action when encountering an armed assailant?" The room was quiet.

"Didarski?"

"Draw your gun?"

"No!" he screamed.

"Francois?"

"Talk to de man?"

"No!" he screamed even louder. "Outman?"

"Freeze?"

"No!" His voice climbed two octaves. Nearby dogs whined in pain. "You freeze and you're a dead man."

Quigley's voice dropped back and he continued. "When confronted by an armed assailant, take cover." His voice rose. "His gun is drawn. Out-drawing him is already impossible and he has a bead on your ass so you can't outshoot him. Your first move is to run, dodge, move, and seek cover. A moving target is harder to hit than a stationary target, and if you decide to stand still and draw your gun ... " Quigley paused, once again composed himself, and continued, " ... if you decide to stand still and draw your gun, he will blow your heart out between your shoulder blades before you can clear leather."

None of us doubted Quigley's words. We were sure he was talking from experience.

"Outman, you've done well so far. Your shooting the past few months has been pretty good. You had experience?"

"Just shooting gophers. There's a bounty on their tails."

"Poor gophers. You ought to have one on yours." Raising his voice an octave, Quigley spoke again. "There's no fun in killing, be it man or beast. No heroics and no pleasure. Killing is highly overstated. Killing has never endowed upon a man one thousandth as much character as saving a life. Outman, you oughta be ashamed. Killing for pleasure or bounty is wrong."

SMALL ARMS TRAINING

"Just putting the poor bugger out of his misery." Recruits are taught to fire at the "centre mass." However, a stray bullet hole might not always count against the recruit.

"But you shot that target in the eye, Corporal," Outman defended himself.

"Just putting the poor bugger out of his misery." Quigley smiled. "Your sidearm is a tool for self-protection and for saving life. Its use is authorized only for that purpose. It is not to stop the escape of a prisoner, it is not to afford you comfort in a dark warehouse, and it is not to be used as a threat. Draw your gun only for the right reason. Be prepared to use it, and recognize that you can only be prepared to use it if you are prepared to kill."

We stood still, taking in his words.

"What part of the body do we shoot at?" Quigley called out.

"Centre mass," a voice replied.

"And why do we shoot?"

"To stop an aggressor capable of inflicting lethal force," Outman replied.

"Good. Don't ever forget those words." Once again Quigley's voice climbed as he drove home our lesson. "We shoot to stop an aggressor and we use lethal force only when confronted by lethal force."

This basic lesson had lasted fifteen minutes, and we were eager to begin target practice. We were always eager to begin target practice, but today was special. For the first time in the four months we had been training, we had been taught why to shoot—not how. From now on our targets were not paper. In our minds they became real.

We all absorbed Corporal Quigley's convincing words—words later needed to answer a question on our final Criminal Law exam. For the moment, however, we were more attracted to punching holes in paper silhouettes than learning the finer points of law.

"Labeau, c'mere."

Francois wheeled his chair up to the firing line.

"Can you stand yet?"

"I tink I can if I got someting to lean on."

"Lean on me, lad. I'll help you. Rumour is that you think you'll graduate from this academy."

"Dat's de rumour, Caporal."

"Here, lean on the post, draw your gun, and shoot that paper bastard till he's dead."

Francois emptied his revolver then sat down, exhausted. The target was inspected and found to contain three holes, none of which were centre mass.

"Focus, Francois, focus," came a whisper from the troop. It was André's voice.

"That sucks, Labeau. You only succeeded in making him mad, and he already wants to kill you. What the hell are you focussing on anyway?"

"De target, Caporal."

"Well, my little friend," Quigley's lips were two inches from Francois' ear, "dat ain't no target. Dat is some son-of-a-bitch who wants to take you out. He don't care if you got a family. He don't care if you got a life. He don't even care if you live. Dat man is gonna kill your sorry ass unless you punch at least two holes in his centre mass—now you stand up and drop that bastard!"

Quigley grabbed Francois by the shoulders and leaned him up against the post. He was not gentle as he slapped his own loaded revolver into Labeau's hand.

"Shoot that bastard, Frenchie, or he'll kill you and your partner!" Quigley screeched. "Shoot!"

BANG. BANG.

Francois levelled two shots at the target, then sat down. His face was covered with sweat from exertion. Corporal Quigley reeled in the target and smiled.

"You get to go home tonight, Constable Labeau. You stopped him. He's dead. You're alive. How does it feel?"

"I don't know, Caporal."

"And God knows, I hope you never will."

During the remainder of the lesson we shot our paper assailants. Quigley was an excellent instructor. When he taught us instinctual shooting, he taught us to focus on the target. When we were required to shoot slowly at a distant target, we were taught to focus on the sights of our revolvers and allow the target to become a blur. Immediately our scores increased by twenty percent.

"Your gun is only a tool and I'm only an instructor. You have the hard task. You must learn."

And we learned. We learned how to shoot, when to shoot, and why shooting was necessary. Most of all, however, Corporal Quigley taught us that there were no heroics in shooting another human. Killing another person was a last resort, an act reserved only for the saving of a life. Quigley did not just teach us to take life—he taught us how to survive.

At the end of our lesson, we were required to wash our hands thoroughly to remove any lead residue. After, Quigley called us back to make a final point. The words that flowed from his mouth shocked each member of our troop.

"The most dangerous gun you will ever face is the one you wear on your hip. The chances of you using it on yourself are ten times greater than the chance of being shot by an assailant." He looked sad and singled out three of us. "Teather, Lumchuck, and Didarski, remember your first duty when you arrived here?"

"Yes, Corporal."

"What was it?"

"We dug a grave, Corporal," Phil answered.

Corporal Quigley's eyes searched out each pair of eyes in our troop, and he seemed to speak to each of us directly. "Don't ever forget that, lads. Don't ever forget that. The person by far the most likely to kill you is yourself. Class dismissed!"

With these startling words firmly planted in our minds, we turned and left the range. From that day forth, each time we touched our revolvers, Quigley's slate-scratching voice would remind us where our real danger lay.

It lay within.

"Everyone has a purpose in life. Even an ignorant, uncaring, and cruel man may serve as an example of how not to behave."

André Bryant

CHAPTER THIRTEEN
Self-defence—Broken Bones
and Other Small Injuries

Wednesday, February 7: It is bizarre how anything repeated often enough begins to seem like the truth—and any pain inflicted long enough becomes not just bearable, but acceptable.

We began to look forward to our half-cooked pancakes and slimy strips of shredded pork flesh almost as much as our powdered milk and artificially flavoured orange crystals.

"Some ting is wrong wit us," Francois said, smiling. "No one is complaining about de food. Do you tink de pancakes are getting better?"

"No, we're getting worse," Outman replied.

"Worse?" Ken Krzyszyk spoke from across the table. "I had to send my tongue out for repairs last week."

Another breakfast had been consumed, but we were yet to realize that for much of our lives we would be inflicted with "Mounties' Eating Disorder." Leisurely meals would be an extraordinary occurrence in our lives. Six months of mess-hall meals conditioned us to eat fast and talk little at mealtime. It would be a habit that would follow us through our lives, a habit few of us would ever break, no matter how hard we tried.

We still had six weeks to endure, and although the end of our road through hell was in sight, there would be more lessons, more torture, and more injuries.

Injuries had become commonplace.

Organized sports awarded us with bruises and sprains, physical education often led to stretched tendons and pulled muscles, and even drill brought its own unique injuries. High brown boots and rough woollen breeches, tightly laced up the calf, wore away all the hair on the back of the lower leg and left most recruits with a telltale localized baldness on their lower legs. Hair in front—bald in back.

Injuries, both major and minor, both painful and inconvenient, were something we had grown to accept. We expected to be injured, and the constant admonishment "tape an aspirin on it" reminded us that our injuries were not severe enough to warrant any serious medical intervention. Injuries were viewed as a sign of progress. Each injury, each bruise, and each sprained joint meant we were one agony closer to graduation.

Each class carried with it both its own range of injuries and its own unique lesson. Some lessons were tougher on the body than others. Self-defence class was the toughest. The reason was simple —our instructor.

We stood, single file, against the wall, watching our self-defence instructor enter the gymnasium. Since our first week in training we had endured the systematic torture applied by this insane individual. Nearly five months of undiluted, agonizing abuse.

During the six months of training, it was not uncommon for a troop to have two or even three instructors for the same class, but an uncaring God had decided to inflict a singular pain upon us all. And the pain had a name: Corporal Franz Leitz.

Corporal Franz Leitz, or Fritz, as he was commonly called, was not quite human. He had introduced himself as a fourth-degree black belt karate master. His first address to our troop focussed on racial purity and physical fitness. Watching Corporal Leitz as he faced our troop, I could still recall his words.

"If I had my way I would shoot you all in the heart and get it over with. Instead, I've been given the privilege of taking you all apart limb from limb, piece by piece, in the next six months. My name is Corporal Fritz Leitz, I am 5'11" tall, I weigh 178 pounds, and I come from pure stock. I can see by looking at you mixed pack of half-breeds that none of you will ever be my physical or mental match. So I'll just do the best I can with each one of you genetic mutants."

Corporal Leitz was proud of his heritage and took great pleasure in challenging us to be as "pure" as he was. He presented himself as a master of several different martial arts, but he made one mistake. He challenged André Byrant, and he was taken to the floor in less than a second.

André had no choice. Leitz had seized him by the windpipe in a move called "the tiger claw," but Bryant had countered with an obscure move from an enigmatic art. He reached back to the side of Leitz's neck with one finger and dropped him to the floor instantly.

André had applied a few ounces of pressure to Leitz's neck to stop his heart and paralyze his diaphragm. No heartbeat and no breathing rendered our "master" unconscious. By the time Leitz's eyeballs had stopped dancing around in their sockets, André had taken his place back with the troop. Leitz staggered to his feet, not quite knowing what had happened.

After that day, Leitz treated us in a more docile manner, but just the same, he continued to be the most brutal of all self-defence instructors. He possessed the world's largest ego, and his vanity showed clearly with each class he taught. Character traits he did not possess, however, were compassion and humour.

No one would ever forget the day when, after a particularly ego-tistical display of his karate skills, he approached Ken Krzyszyk.

"Do you know why they call me the cat, Krzyszyk?" he asked, hoping to be complimented on his agility and speed.

"Because you pee in a sandbox, Corporal?" Ken replied.

Five minutes later, Krzyszyk regained consciousness.

One memorable day, only six weeks from the end of our training, we learned a wonderful self-defence technique, but Corporal Leitz was not the teacher.

With his chest puffed out, his spine superbly straight, and his cranium completely vacant, Leitz addressed our troop.

"Today I will teach you how to avoid becoming a landowner," he said loudly. "Do you know what a landowner is?"

"No, Corporal."

"Lumchuck, front and centre!" he yelled. Larry stepped four paces out from the troop, turned left, and jerked to attention.

"At ease."

Lumchuck raised his left leg, slammed it down onto the polished tile floor, and placed his hands behind his back.

Leitz smiled. This target was too easy. Bringing his left leg up, he snapped a kick that stopped a mere inch short of Lumchuck's groin. "If I kick you there, you are the instant owner of two acres and they will ache for days. Wanna be a landowner, Lumchuck?"

"No, Corporal."

"Then listen up. I'll show you how to avoid it."

He had our undivided attention.

"The pukes, the creeps, the gutter slime that you will be dealing with in a dark alley won't see you as a person. Nosiree, lads, when they come on the attack, they won't be fighting by the Marquis of Queensberry rules. They won't give you first hit, they won't fight clean, and they won't hesitate to hit below the belt. When a puke wants to fight you he places an imaginary bull's-eye on your groin, then kicks for the best score he can acquire. When that happens, you will drop like the sacks of excrement that you are. You'll puke your guts out and you'll spend a week cuddling with an ice pack. But that doesn't matter. Do you know what matters?"

"No, Corporal," we answered.

"What matters is you lost the fight. And losing is not an option." Corporal Leitz smiled, turned his attention toward Lumchuck, and said confidently, "Kick me, fat boy."

"I've lost twenty-five pounds, Corporal."

"I don't care if your mother has cancer or not. I want your attention. Kick me, fat boy, and you know what to aim for."

"But ..." Larry stammered.

"Fatchuck, if you don't kick me between the legs in the next two seconds, I'll pin a picture of your mother on that leather punching bag in the corner and put up a sign that says 'Hit the whore—five cents a whack!'"

Lumchuck's face flushed red with anger. Then, as the blood drained away, his leg snapped forward and found its mark.

Thuck.

Leitz thrust his pelvis forward and allowed Lumchuck's kick to land home, but he barely flinched.

"Lads, if you have the guts to thrust your hips forward, to present your groin to the enemy, his kick will not hurt you."

We stood in shock as he continued his explanation.

"Thrust forward and his foot will overshoot its mark and land square on your perineum. Do you know what your perineum is, Lumchuck?"

"No, Corporal."

"It's your taint!" He stepped forward and yelled into Larry's face. In the fresh morning light, we watched as tiny flecks of saliva propelled themselves from Leitz's mouth onto Lumchuck's face. Shout-spitting on recruits was a right that many of our instructors enjoyed. In that very singular manner we had all become intimate with our instructors. We shared body fluids.

"You don't know what your taint is, Lumchuck?" he repeated.

"No, Corporal, I don't know what my taint is."

"I'll tell you." Leitz turned to face the troop. "Your taint is that area down low and between your legs that taint your bum hole and taint your family collectibles. Your taint can take a licking and keep on ticking." He smiled, and we wondered just what he had meant by that last comment.

"If you have the guts to tilt your pelvis toward your opponent's foot, he'll overshoot his mark and your worst discomfort will be a bruised taint."

"What if I merely blocked the kick, Corporal?"

"You mean like we showed you during your first month of training?"

"Yes."

"You just kicked my taint. Do I look hurt?"

"No, Corporal," Lumchuck answered, not knowing where this conversation would end.

"Okay, Lumpy Larry, assume the position."

Larry reached down toward his groin and crossed his arms at the wrist. We had been taught to defend our private possessions using the crossed-wrist technique early in our training, and it had seemed a reasonable defence.

"You ready, fat boy?"

"Yes, Corporal."

Smack. Corporal Leitz's foot flew up, hit Lumchuck's wrists, and returned to the floor. Larry's form was impeccable, and it succeeded in stopping our instructor's foot. His form had protected his most valued possessions. But his perfect form had left him with one broken finger. Lumchuck fell to his knees, holding his left hand close to his stomach. He groaned.

"Get up, you bloated chunk of rippling flesh."

Lumchuck did not respond, and Leitz closed the distance and grabbed him by the throat. The upward force applied by Corporal Leitz raised him to a standing position.

"Now you listen up, fat boy." His eyes glanced over Larry's shoulder and met ours as he continued. "You never go down and give up on a fight unless you're dead or unconscious. When you give up, that's when that useless piece of garbage takes your gun and caps you. Getting capped means lying dead in the alley with half your head blown away." We had hated Leitz, but he was starting to make sense, and we listened intently as his eyes looked deep into our souls. "No!" he shouted. "You will never give up fighting unless you are unconscious or dead. As long as you draw breath, as long as you can think, and as long as you can move, you will fight that no-good-gutter-crawling-better-off-dead-than-us piece of crap until you win the fight. We don't lose fights in this Force unless we're dead or comatose. We don't let the creeps take our lives in alleys and we don't let them make our girlfriends sad and our wives widows. No asshole is ever gonna take my gun away from me unless he breaks it outta my dead and bloodied hand."

Leitz stopped, moved face-to-face with Lumchuck and yelled, "Is that clear Lumchuck—I said is that ... "

"Yes, Corporal!" Larry screamed back, momentarily interrupting the instructor's verbal attack.

"Yes, Corporal!" Lumchuck screamed again. Leitz's eyes grew large, surprised by meek Larry's aggressiveness. "I ain't never gonna give up to any gutter-crawlin-scummy-bastard, and I ain't gonna give up to you. You want another crack at me before I take you apart?"

We were in shock. Leitz was clearly crazy. He had demonstrated that many times. His views on racial purity and the many beatings he had handed out to us individually, under the guise of recruit training, had showed him to be unquestionably abnormal. He was a violent, aggressive creature who took great pleasure in inflicting pain on recruits who remained submissive. Larry was volunteering for a death sentence.

"Can you hear me, Corporal? I'm talking to you. You want to do it now or ain't you got the guts. Go ahead, Corporal. Take your best freakin' shot before I slam-dunk you so hard, your brains and your arsehole will be living a week and a half apart. Go ahead. I've got the surprise of a century just bloody well waiting for you. C'mon. C'mon, Corporal. This Jew-boy you roughed up last month is gonna kick ass and he's gonna kick your ass. Go ahead, Corporal, make your move and I'll rip your freakin' arm off and beat you to death with the bloody end. Go ahead, Corporal— I'm waiting."

Leitz stood in shock for a full thirty seconds while the verbal attack grew in intensity. Finally, Lumchuck had stopped shout-spitting in Leitz's face. Their eyes were locked, staring deep into each other's being.

Silence.

We could hear our hearts pounding. Everyone in the troop expected the fight of the millennium.

Everyone except Lumchuck.

And André Bryant.

More silence. Neither combatant flinched.

Leitz broke the silence first as he pulled his gaze away from our hero, Constable Lumchuck.

"Well done, Constable," Leitz said softly but firmly. "Well done. Take your place."

Larry returned to his position in the troop and we heard him whisper to André, "Thanks again, buddy. Thanks again."

"Shita Wassa," André whispered as he winked at Larry.

"Shita Wassa," Larry replied quietly.

"Okay, you big bunch of sissies. You tiny insignificant miscreants. What you just saw was one man—the only man in the troop—with the guts to earn the title Constable. He was wounded and he knew he didn't stand a chance against my mastery of the martial arts. He knew he had already lost so what did he do? I'll tell you what he did. He came on the attack. There ain't no scumbucket in the world that would attack a crazy man like "Lumchuck and ... " Leitz presented Lumchuck with a rare compliment—the only compliment that was ever conferred upon our troop by him." ... Lumchuck, I'll never know if you were ready to fight me or not, but after seeing you go crazoid, I didn't want to find out. If I'm ever in a fight, I'd consider your backup as my good fortune."

Lumchuck smiled ever so slightly. He had won. He had beaten Leitz at his own game. He had earned the respect of our self-defence instructor, but one more troopmate was about to be tested.

"Bryant."

"Yes, Corporal."

"I hear you know how to fight."

"Everyone knows how to fight, Corporal. Some of us do it better than others."

"Yeah? Well, did you know I could rip your guts out with a rolled-up newspaper?"

"Yes, Corporal."

"Yes, Corporal," Leitz mocked. "Can you do better?"

"Yes, Corporal."

Fritz's eyes grew large—again. We had nearly become accustomed to shocking him.

"How?" Leitz asked.

"You need a whole newspaper. I could kill you with just one page."

"How you gonna do that?"

"Easy, Corporal. Just submit the photo I took of you last week to the local newspaper."

"Photo?"

POLISH THE PLANE!

Sitting proudly on base is the shell of CF-MPH, a Beechcraft D18S airplane waiting for the ultimate service. Purchased by the RCMP in 1946 and placed into "Northern Service," this aircraft was turned over to the Canadian Armed Forces at the outbreak of the Second World War. Whether it be self-defence, drill or even law class, any error committed by a recruit would bring an admonishment of "Do you want to polish the plane?" No one ever volunteered for this duty.

"Yup. The picture I took of you coming out of Carolyn's house. You know, the house with the red light in the window. I'm sure the Regina *Free Press* would like that. Heck, Corporal, one page of newspaper and your marriage, your children, your house, and your job would disappear. No pension, no family, no job. You're a pretty proud man, Corporal. You'd probably eat your gun." Leitz's face blushed. "I'd say that would be killing you with just one sheet of newspaper, wouldn't you?"

"Class dismissed," Leitz called out in a less-than-aggressive manner. Once again he had been beaten, yet he would not acknowledge defeat. As we passed by him in single file, André's voice was heard to say, "Shita Wassa."

"Shita Wassa," Lumchuck softly answered back.

"Lumchuck," Leitz called.

"Yes, Corporal."

"Your finger."

"What about it, Corporal?" Larry's finger had begun to swell and turn blue, but he would not acknowledge the pain.

"Tape an aspirin on it."

"Yes, Corporal."

Compared to our self-defence class, the rest of the day passed by as a boring succession of classroom lectures, swimming, marching, and more classroom lectures.

Larry visited the post hospital during lunch hour and Doctor Death splinted his finger. No X-rays were taken—treatment consisted simply of the administration of a small metal splint and a small bottle of aspirins. Larry missed lunch.

Cream soup. But we never found out just what had been creamed.

Later that evening after another supper at the Mystery Meat Cafe, we sat together in our dormitory, perfecting the spit-shine on our high brown boots.

"André," Ken Krzyszyk asked. "What the heck is this Shita Wassa thing you and beluga-brain were whispering?"

"Shita Wassa." André smiled. "It's an ancient Chinese martial art."

"Who was it named after?" Ken asked.

"No one. Shita Wassa is the title of the art." André continued. "Shita Wassa uses the most powerful force known to mankind. It is the most misunderstood and the least used tool we have at our command."

"Tool?"

"Yes, tool. This tool has the ability to hurt or heal, to injure or soothe, to attack or defend. This tool is ..."

"Your words," Ken jumped in.

"Your words," André confirmed.

"What does Shita Wassa mean?"

"The Tongue Technique."

We all smiled. Larry Lumchuck had beaten Leitz without touching him. He had used the most powerful tool known to mankind: words.

"Works pretty good, too," Larry added. He held up his splinted finger and, in jest, showed us an aspirin he had taped to the end of the splint. "At least you don't break a finger defending yourself."

"Damn that Leitz. All he wants to do is show off his skills and inflict injuries on us. He's the most useless piece of flesh I've ever seen," Ken Krzyszyk said.

"His skills aren't that good," André said, then added, "Besides, he ain't really useless."

"Oh. Tell me what use that dork has in our lives." Ken challenged André to come up with a reasonable answer.

"Everyone has a purpose in life. Even an ignorant, uncaring, and cruel man may serve as an example, to teach others how not to behave."

That night we turned our lights out and slept peacefully. Our dragon had been defeated. We had won.

Troop 18 ruled!

> "First aid is merely the art of keeping someone alive with superficial activity until God decides whether or not they will live."
>
> Corporal Jocelyn Ribeault

CHAPTER FOURTEEN
First Aid—Wooden Splints and Soft-Boiled Eggs

Thursday, February 22: With only five weeks left in our six-month basic training, we felt inspired. No one had failed any tests, and only one major barracks inspection lay ahead. Although Thursday nights would still be reserved for routine stand-to inspections, our last formal inspection would take place tonight. Corps Sergeant Major Bilby, accompanied by the commanding officer of Depot and led by corporals Wheeler and Withers, would review our dormitory.

As we gagged down our morning pancakes, our apprehension became obvious.

"We got enough floor polish?" Outman asked.

"Yeah," Didarski answered. "I bought a can yesterday."

"Spray bottles?" another voice asked.

"Yup. Got them locked up in my gun drawer. We don't have to worry about vinegar." We laughed as Ken pinched his nose, avoiding an imaginary smell.

"What about our boots? Sure would like a shine like Wheeler has on his boots. Anybody know how he does that?" Burl asked.

"Yes. I have a surprise for everyone tonight. We'll have the best boots on the base," André said, sporting his three-C aura of cool, calm, and courage.

"What? How we gonna do that? You got a trick up your sleeve? What if we get caught?" Burl asked, reverting back to his normal state of paranoia.

"Tonight we shine," was all that André would say.

"Better be good, André," Outman said.

"It is," he replied.

Ten minutes later we had pounded down breakfast and reported to our final first-aid class.

For five months we had practised applying traction splints to broken bones, direct pressure to severed arteries, and mouth-to-mouth resuscitation to a rubber dummy affectionately known as Resusci-Anne.

"Good thing they don't make us practise on a Resusci-George," Don Outman had said during our first class. That comment had lost him a week's freedom.

Corporal Jocelyn Ribeault, our first-aid instructor, had set the stage during the first five minutes of our initial lesson.

"I don't care if your victims are male, female, black, white, or red," he said. "They will probably be blue from lack of oxygen and it is your duty to bring them back to life. If anyone here has a problem with saving a life because of race, gender, or any other trait, step forward and I'll hand you your marching orders."

"Marching orders" was a euphemism for immediate discharge.

No one stepped forward.

We gathered in the first-aid hall, eager to pass our final exam by demonstrating our lifesaving skills to our instructor. We knew he would demand perfection, and we were prepared to give him what he asked for. We listened as Corporal Ribeault dispensed his instructions.

"Didarski, lie down in the corner. You have a compound, protruding fracture of your left femur. I want to hear some groaning from you."

Phil did as ordered, screaming and moaning so loud Corporal Dunsel interrupted his law class next door to see who had been hurt.

"Labeau, you're his only chance. You'll find everything you need over there." Corporal Ribeault pointed to the opposite corner of the room where a large plastic garbage can held all the necessary supplies. "C'mon, lad, he's dying."

Phil's moaning increased in pitch and intensity. He held his imaginary wound and screamed loudly. "Help me! I'm dying! Helllp meee!" Didarski was a good actor.

Quickly, Francois wheeled his chair to the corner, reached down into the can, and picked up two traction splints and a handful of triangular cloth bandages. No one helped him.

This was his test.

Wheeling back to Phil Didarski, Labeau launched himself from his wheelchair and landed face-down at Didarski's feet. Rolling over, he began to position the wood splints.

"C'mon, man, he's dying. Hurry up."

"You tink you could make yourself useful, Caporal? You tink instead of standing dere, you could call an ambulance?"

"Good move, Labeau." Corporal Ribeault turned to the class. "Take control. Direct others to help you. You can't do it all yourself."

"Labeau, he's only got three minutes to live. What can you do for him?"

"Well, I tink I could soft-boil him an egg," Labeau answered, still tying the splint in place, losing no time whatsoever.

We exploded into laughter. Corporal Ribeault lost control and laughed with us. Then he turned back to Francois.

"He's near death. Going into shock. Whatchya gonna do?" In an attempt to add realism to the test, Corporal Ribeault changed the conditions, adding a new complication.

"Lumchuck," Francois ordered, "go to de cloakroom and bring me two storm coats. Dis man's in shock. Got to keep him warm."

"Good," Ribeault complimented him.

"You gonna stand dere, Caporal, or you gonna go and get dis man an ambulance?" Francois countered as he finished tying the splint.

"That's it? You finished?" Corporal Ribeault asked.

"No, Caporal. When I am finished with dis patient, I will tell you." Reaching into his pocket, he retrieved an aspirin and a small piece of transparent tape. Without slowing down, Francois taped an aspirin onto the side of his patient's splint, then looked up at his instructor.

"Dere, Caporal. Dis man will survive. I sure am glad dat he only had a broken leg. If he had been pregnant I would have had a bad problem."

"How so?" Ribeault asked.

"I only got one aspirin."

Again the troop erupted into laughter and Corporal Ribeault joined us.

"You pass, Francois," Corporal Ribeault said as he tried to control his laughter. "You did just fine."

"Tank you, Caporal."

"Want a hand getting back into your wheelchair?"

"No tanks, Caporal. De wheelchair is only for sympathy. I don't tink I'll be needing it forever." We were surprised as we watched him drag himself over to his wheelchair. Grasping the arms, he raised himself, spun around, and sat down. It was as if his legs were actually helping him. Was this possible? Had Labeau actually used his legs?

No one knew, except Francois.

And André.

"Okay, Didarski, you're healed. Untie yourself and take your place with the troop."

Phil looked at the bandages and the aspirin and smiled.

"Krzyszyk, you're next."

"Yes, Corporal."

"See that?" Corporal Ribeault pointed toward the Resusci-Anne dummy.

"Yes, Corporal."

"She's dead. No life signs. No breathing. No pulse. Pupils fixed and dilated. Whatchya gonna do?"

"I'm gonna call Francois' priest. Seems giving the last rites to a dying man worked fine for him."

Again we laughed, and Francois laughed the hardest.

"Okay, smartass, you got less than a minute to take action."

Kneeling beside his rubber victim, Ken spoke calmly, maintaining his composure. "First I check for breathing." He held his ear to her mouth. "No breathing. Next I check for pulse." Lightly he laid his fingers alongside her trachea. "She's either dead or my watch has stopped." We laughed, but Ken was serious. "No pulse," he said, loud enough for our instructor to hear. "Now I go to work." Expressing himself in a confident manner, Ken spoke into Resusci-Anne's ear. "Anne, I am a police officer, and you will be okay. I am going to help you breathe."

We had been trained to take five seconds to reassure our victims— even the unconscious victims. Hearing is the last sense to leave before profound unconsciousness takes over, and as Ken whispered words of assurance into Annie's ear, the story that Corporal Ribeault had told us nearly five months earlier came back.

"She was only ten years old when I pulled her limp body from the lake. I whispered words of assurance into her ear and began cardiopulmonary resuscitation. Several hours later, the doctors finished the resuscitation procedure at the hospital. The young girl I had pulled from the lake had regained consciousness, and I learned why we are taught to take this time." He continued his explanation. "Only one day after I had removed her lifeless body from the water, I sat beside her bed. She spoke words I will not forget." He looked in our eyes as we listened to his tale. "'It was a close one for you,' I told her. Then she whispered the words I want to pass on to you today.

"'I wasn't worried,' she said. 'I was in a dark place, but a policeman kept telling me I was going to be okay. Policemen always tell the truth, so I decided to come back.'"

Ken repeated his promise. "I am a police officer and you are going to be okay." Then he added, "How about a three-minute egg?"

"Get with the program, Krzyszyk," Ribeault ordered.

Quickly Ken placed his lips on the dummy, inflated the lungs three times, and continued to depress the chest with the heel of his hands while counting. "One thousand and one, one thousand and two, one thousand and three ..." When he had counted to "one thousand and five," he once again inflated Annie's lungs.

"Corporal," he called, "you gonna stand around on me like you did to Labeau, or you gonna make yourself useful and call an ambulance? One thousand and one ..." He continued the chest compressions.

Krzyszyk carried on with the chest compressions and lung inflations for another five minutes before being advised that he had passed his test.

"That's it, Krzyszyk. You've pumped her long enough. If I left you there any longer, you might become emotionally involved."

"Where's my ambulance, Corporal?"

"You're pushing it, Krzyszyk. I said the test is over."

"Yes, Corporal."

"Oh, one more thing," Ribeault added.

"Yes, Corporal?"

"Where's the aspirin?"

"It's in the ambulance," Ken said, and we all laughed.

Our test continued for the remainder of the morning. More compound fractures, more drownings, and more whispers in patients' ears filled the hours. Each member of our troop served as both victim and rescuer as Corporal Ribeault graded our actions.

"Not bad, lads. Not bad at all. I might even be persuaded to say you all did well."

"Tank you, Caporal." Labeau spun his wheelchair around in a victory salute and lightly slapped Ribeault on the back. "Tank you, Caporal, and on behalf of our troop we all tank you for your help dis past five months."

"You're welcome, lads," Ribeault said, only slightly annoyed from Francois' too-familiar slap on his back. "I will see you all receive a passing grade, but before you leave my classroom I want you to take in one more lesson. It's a short one, but I want it to be the lesson most remembered."

We stood and listened as he continued.

"First aid is not a miracle activity. In your careers, many of you will look death in the face as your attempt to breathe life back into a victim fails. You do not have the power over life and death ..." His face grew serious. "... that is reserved for a Higher Power. God. First aid is merely the act of keeping someone alive with superficial activity until God decides whether or not they will live." Then his voice took on an even more serious tone. "It is you who must survive, physically, emotionally, and spiritually. Any man who pulls a lifeless body from a lake, river, swamp, or swimming pool had best remember this." He raised his voice and continued, "The person you recover is already dead. If, by good fortune and quick cardiopulmonary resuscitation, their life is restored, that's a bonus. If they remain lifeless ..." Corporal Ribeault looked out the window. His face grew sad, and the lines on his forehead suggested he was speaking from experience, not his instructor's manual. "... if they remain lifeless, you must bear no burden at the end of your shift. Know you have done your best." Then, still looking out the window, he added, "Remember, please, that their death was not your fault. Their fate was decided not by your failure, but by a Higher Power. I hope that thought will afford some of you peace."

Silence.

"Any questions?

"No, Corporal."

"Good."

"Caporal?" Francois asked.

"Yes?"

"Once again, Caporal—thanks."

"Class dismissed."

Corporal Ribeault left the class ahead of us. He had taught us how to use pressure to stop bleeding, how to whisper to dead people, and generally how to save lives. We all smiled as he walked ahead of us, and we continued to smile as we watched him walk down the hallway. Taped firmly between his shoulder blades, on the back of his shirt, for all to see, was—an aspirin.

He would recover. Labeau had seen to that.

Five minutes later, we stared at our lunch and wondered if we would also survive.

"What's dis fuzzy stuff on de meat?" Francois asked.

"Penicillin. It'll do you good," Lumchuck replied.

"And de vegetables?"

None of us had ever seen blue vegetables before. But we ate them just the same. They tasted like pancakes.

That afternoon was designated as free time. No classes were scheduled, but our so-called liberty was spent preparing for our last formal inspection.

"Okay, André. What's the big secret? How are we gonna get a shine on our high browns to match Corporal Wheeler's?" Harold asked. He had no doubt worried about his boots all day.

"Easy." André passed out five tins of shoe polish and a box of candles.

"Okay, so we're gonna shine our boots all night?"

"Look at the tin," André suggested.

"Parade Wax," Ken read the words out loud. "What's this? Where'd you get it?"

"Easy," André replied. "I followed Wheeler to town last week and watched him enter the Wascanna Shoe Renew. Once he left, I walked up to the counter and said 'I'll have what he had.' The lady gave me a tin of this Parade Wax, so I asked for four more. Two weeks ago, while on fatigues, I was given an envelope to deliver to Corporal Wheeler's office. I was happy to see the office empty, and I took a few minutes to scout around."

"You mean spy?" Phil accused.

"Okay, spy." André smiled. "Well, I saw a soft shoe brush, a small box of soft rags, a tin of Parade Wax, and a candle."

"More Ninja shit, eh?" Outman laughed.

"Yeah. It's easy, gentlemen. I've got it all figured out. We smear the Parade Wax on our shoes, melt it in with the candles, and buff it up with a soft cloth."

Ten minutes later our troop had the shiniest boots on the base.

"Master Ninja, you've done it again," someone called out to André.

"Naw, it's just a matter of advantage management. I took the advantage to scout out Wheeler's office, and I managed to use the occasion constructively. Advantage management." He smiled as he spoke the words.

We shone all our shoes that afternoon. Our high brown boots, our ankle boots, our issue oxfords, and even our civilian shoes all exhibited a mirror shine.

We washed the walls, ironed the bedsheets, and picked our scarlet tunics free of the most minute lint particles. We were prepared to pass the tightest inspection possible. We washed the washroom floor and polished the walls and the mirrors. We scrubbed the toilets twice and flushed them ten times. We placed new toilet paper rolls on the hangers and folded each of the ends neatly to form a triangle. Nothing foreign remained. Not a whisker, not a hair, and not a hint of anything that could bring failure contaminated that washroom.

We did not attend the mess for supper that evening. Inspection would be conducted at twenty hundred hours and we needed every minute to prepare.

Fifteen minutes before inspection, we carefully took up position by our beds. Thirty-two scarlet tunics and thirty-two pairs of mirror-polished high brown boots awaited the most stringent of inspections. We waited in silence and stared at the floor that we had polished to a mirror shine. To avoid scuff marks from our boots, we had wrapped the soles of our high browns with soft rags. As we walked over the buffed surface of the linoleum, we left no telltale marks. Once each man took his place by the foot of his bed, he removed the soft rags and stuffed them into the pockets of his breeches.

Francois sat in his wheelchair at the foot of his bed; then, at the last minute, he pushed his chair backwards, opened his closet door, and retrieved two crutches. Carefully and slowly, he made his way back to the foot of his bed and stood tall.

"Way to go, Francois," Outman called out.

"Yo, Francois. Good man," another voice added.

"Yay, Ninja!" several others cheered.

"They're coming," Phil called out. Footsteps echoed off the stairs leading to our dorm.

The double doors opened and Corporal Wheeler, followed by Corporal Withers and Corps Sergeant Major Bilby, entered the room. Our commanding officer followed close behind.

"Sir," Corporal Wheeler announced, "may I present to you the members of Troop 18, ready for your inspection."

Without acknowledging the introduction or speaking a word, Bilby commenced his inspection. Walking slowly, he scrutinized our clothing, our grooming, and our pits. Each recruit withstood a thirty-second examination from cold eyes that probed every inch of his clothing and body.

"You have a pimple on the back of your neck," Bilby said to Outman.

"Yes, sir."

"Fix it."

"Yes, sir."

"Labeau, your crutches aren't straight."

"Yes, sir," Francois replied, bringing his left crutch closer to his body.

"That's better, lad. If you're gonna stand—then you're gonna stand at attention."

"Yes, sir."

Bilby continued, taking us on individually as Corporal Wheeler followed one step behind, ready to note any imperfections on his clipboard.

"Didarski." He stood face-to-face with Phil.

"Yes, sir?"

"Your girlfriend?"

"It's over, sir."

"Sorry. Good luck on a new start, young man."

"Thank you, sir."

"Someday you'll find yourself a good lady who really loves you, and you'll be passing out cigars instead of fighting over them."

"Yes, sir."

"By the way, Didarski, you got that ear fixed yet?"

"No, sir."

"Fix it. We can't have you attending Pass Out with one ear bigger than the other."

"Yes, sir."

"Krzyszyk."

"Sir?"

"How the hell do you pronounce that?"

"Kerzisik, sir."

"Whatever. Change your name."

"Yes, sir."

"Burl."

"Yes, sir."

"You from Toronto?"

"Yes, sir."

"Too bad."

"Lumchuck."

"Yes, sir."

"You're wasting away. You've lost so much weight if you drank a glass of tomato juice on a cold day you'd look like a thermometer." Then he added quietly, "Congratulations, young man. Forty-two pounds?"

"Yes, sir. Forty-two pounds." Larry thrust his chest out farther.

"Sorry to hear about your mother, Larry. You have done well—very well."

"Yes, sir." Larry's eyes filled with tears. Being addressed by his first name by our CSM, combined with the worry of his mother's illness, was too much. Her health had improved, but her fate was still uncertain.

"Steady up, Constable," Bilby said softly.

"Yes, sir."

Corps Sergeant Major Bilby continued the inspection. It had become obvious that our instructors reported directly to him and kept him informed about every aspect of our history and progress. He knew us all personally, and as our training neared its end, he spoke to us both as individuals and as a troop.

"Corporal Withers?" Bilby called.

"Sir."

"I understand this troop has given us some grief a while ago."

"Yes, sir."

"And the nature of that grief was ...?"

"They weren't a troop yet, sir. Just a loose collection of rabble."

"And now?"

"Sir, like Corporal Wheeler, I am also pleased to present to you, Troop 18. We have a fine troop here, sir. A troop that I would be proud to call my own."

Thirty-two chests enlarged and thirty-two spines straightened. For the first time in six months, we shared the same emotion: pride.

"Yes, sir—we have a fine troop here," Don Withers repeated.

"Nice boots, also," Bilby remarked. "What are you using on your leather, Bryant?"

"Parade Wax, sir," André replied.

"How'd you find out about Parade Wax?"

André blushed, then replied, "I saw a can of it on Corporal Wheeler's desk, sir, and he has the best boots on base."

"Has he now?"

"Uh, next to yours, sir."

"Sucking up to the Corps Sergeant Major just might get you somewhere, Bryant."

André smiled.

"But not today."

André stopped smiling.

One hour later the inspection drew to a close. Every corner and

FIRST AID?

First-aid class had prepared us for almost anything—almost! From Scarlet Tunic, Volume 2, *Corporal Teather is pictured "rescuing" over 100 chickens from sure death. The chickens were later adopted out as pets.*

every surface had been inspected for dust. Haircuts had been closely examined, and three more pimples had been located and documented on Wheeler's clipboard.

Walking to the end of the dormitory, Corps Sergeant Major Bilby spoke loudly: "Troop 18, stand aaat eeeaaassse!" In one thunderous clap, thirty-two legs raised and slammed down hard on the linoleum as we realigned ourselves with feet shoulder-width apart.

Thirty-two legs.

Francois, although barely raising his leg from the floor, managed to follow the direction in sync with the troop.

"Well done, Labeau." Bilby almost smiled. "Well done, lad."

"Troop 18, I have something to say to you, and until the day of your graduation ceremony—your pass out—this will be the last time we will speak." Corporals Wheeler and Withers stood by his side, standing at attention—staring directly ahead.

"Five months ago you arrived here on this base. I watched from my window as scruffy, long-haired, undisciplined individuals walked by my office on the way to the post barber. You have all changed. It was our intent to bring you into the Royal Canadian Mounted Police and mould—some would call it brainwash—you into what you are today. I see we have succeeded."

We were beginning to understand the torture, the punishment, and the discipline that had been inflicted upon us for the past five months, and I watched several heads nod in agreement. I joined them.

"Few people will ever understand what you have been through. Oh, there are a few groups—the U.S. Navy Seals, the Green Berets, perhaps one or two Canadian military groups—that have gone through a similar transformation, but let me make one thing very clear to you, lads."

We waited.

"You are unique. Your training, your experience here, and your transformation is one rarely copied elsewhere. Your families and the friends you shared before you came here will say that you have changed. That is the truth. None will understand what you have been through, and if you tell your stories, tell them well, lest you be called foolish by the nonbelievers or the uncaring. Let this change reflect in a positive manner for the remainder of your lives. And ..."

CSM Bilby paused as he made eye contact with each member of the troop.

"And ... I wish you all a long life, gentlemen."

He referred to us as "gentlemen." We had never been addressed with any term of respect since the day of our arrival. For the past five months we had been called "ladies," "rabble," "rab," "children," "wimps," "dozy little men," and "cretins."

But gentlemen?

We had changed.

"Troop 18!" Bilby bellowed."Aaatenshuun!"

Thirty-two spit-shone boots slammed down hard on the green and black linoleum. I was not sure, but even Francois seemed to raise his leg higher and let his foot drop more firmly onto the floor.

Bilby's "Aaatenshuun" still echoed off the walls as he turned and left our dorm. In silence we listened as the precise staccato sound made by three sets of feet faded away.

The room stayed quiet.

"We did it," a voice whispered.

"We did it," another voice replied, louder.

"Troop 18 rules!" Ken Krzyszyk yelled.

"We can do dat!" Francois yelled even louder.

That night we dined by candlelight, for the last time.

Inspector Chicken and imported wine.

"It's not whether you win or lose ... it's how you hold the trophy."

Gerry Milligan

CHAPTER FIFTEEN
Murder Ball Victory—Blood, Sweat, and Beers

Friday, March 22: As the senior troop on base we were granted certain privileges. Fatigues were only a memory, and although we were obliged to rise at reveille and attend morning parade, it was our troop that handed out the toilet brushes and brass polish.

Troop 19 stood at attention in the drill hall and looked at us as we delegated them to the base toilets. Displeasure showed on their faces.

"Know what you can do with this brush, bristles included?" a Troop 19 smart mouth sneered at Lumchuck.

"You take this brush or I'll ram it so far up your nose your eyes will stay crossed for a week."

"Think you're tough enough?" came another voice from the junior troop.

"I know we're tough enough," Didarski answered.

Troop 19 was the biggest, toughest, and meanest troop that Depot had seen in years. They had formed up just two weeks after us, and although they were designated as our junior troop, they resisted our help and ignored our advice. It was as though they were hand-picked for their obstinance and recruited to terrorize all other troops. Their reputation, established during their first two months, was a bad one. Their nighttime raids on other dormitories and their verbal threats had made life miserable for many troops. They had alienated their group from other recruits, and they had earned little respect from their instructors.

They were rebels, a troop of individuals. We had become an individual troop.

"Yes," André Bryant stepped in. "I think we're big enough. How's about a game of Murder Ball tonight? Nineteen hundred hours in the riding stable. You and us. Sudden death. No rules. No witnesses. First team to score wins."

"What about your cripple? He gonna be the ball?"

"You just worry about yourselves, lads." André spoke his insult softly, then screamed louder than any instructor in the history of Depot. "Now you clean them toilets with your brushes or we'll clean 'em with your freakin' heads."

"Tonight." The word came from a mutant in the back row.

"Tonight," André answered.

"Bring your cripple, we'll use him as the ball." Smart Mouth took a final shot at Francois, and Troop 19 laughed as they took their brushes and marched toward "A" block, their assigned toilets. As Smart Mouth, the last defiant recruit, walked out the door, Francois swung his wheelchair around quickly and caught his rival's ankle with the metal footrest. The sound of metal tearing into flesh was sickening. In one move, Francois had levelled the playing field.

"Pick yourself up, lad," Francois said. "I tink you have to learn to walk before you can play Murder Ball."

"Tonight," the recruit said as he limped away.

"*Ce soir*," Francois added in French. "*Ce soir, mon ami*— tonight, my friend."

Two hours later we sat in our dormitory, confirming our day's activities. Corporal Wheeler had promised us two hours of drill before noon. The afternoon would be taken up with self-defence and swimming. Our graduation demonstrations (our Pass Out) were to be the crowning achievement of our six months' imprisonment.

It was to be perfect.

"What about de Murder Ball tonight?" Francois said. "I tink we maybe bit off more dan we can chew."

"They made one mistake," André said.

"What?" several voices joined in.

"No rules. They agreed to that."

"No rules? They'll kill us," Burl complained.

"No." André smiled. "Here's what we'll do ..."

With a plan in our hearts and a smile on our faces, we reported to the drill hall. Today we would practise perfection—and tonight, we would kick butt.

"Okay, ladies, we're gonna teach you some tricky moves today." We had grown relaxed with Corporal Wheeler's name-calling, and he shared our laughter. Wheeler was joined by Corporal Withers, who also addressed our troop.

"I've never seen perfection before, ladies." Withers emphasized the last word. "Am I gonna see it today?"

"Yes, Corporal." Thirty-two voices rang out. Francois sat in his wheelchair but proudly wore his high brown boots, riding breeches, and scarlet tunic. He did not take part in our drill exercises, but he always attended. The Force had still not decided his fate. Francois had passed all academic subjects and had developed admirable upper body strength, but his legs remained too weak to support him without crutches.

For two hours we marched, slammed our feet down on the wooden floor, and saluted. Under Corporal Wheeler's guidance we learned two new marching patterns that had never been attempted at graduation. One required the troop to split into equal sections, then intertwine as we marched to form a moving intersection of bodies. The other, even more complex drill was a manoeuvre whereby the troop split once again into two halves. Each section marched around the perimeter of the drill hall, but in opposite directions. At Wheeler's command, our circles gradually closed rank, shrinking until it became impossible to continue. Then, as if by magic, a hole opened up and the two sections emerged from virtual chaos, marching as one solid mass of scarlet tunics. An individual troop.

As impossible as this manoeuvre seemed, Wheeler's directions made it easy. Nearly two hours into our rehearsal, our legs ached, our feet were blistered, and our heads pounded from the tight, rigid Stetsons, but we kept marching. And Wheeler encouraged us.

"When you're one troop, one mind, one purpose, you can accomplish anything," he called out over our footsteps. "You can do it. Keep marching. You officers aren't followers, you are leaders. You are the best flamin' troop this base has ever seen. You are setting a standard for others to follow. You are leaders." With each compliment, our spines grew straighter, our chests larger, and our marching more precise.

"You, gentlemen, are leaders!" he called out loudly. "You are not following tradition today, you are making it!" he screamed at the top of his lungs. "And ..." his voice grew loud and clear, "as sure as God made little green apples and Inspector Chicken, you will succeed."

Cadence was lost. Our troop collapsed. Laughter and shock took over. He knew.

Corporals Wheeler and Withers stood together at the front of the drill hall. Smiling. They knew!

"Steady up, gentlemen," Withers called, pretending to be serious, but we continued laughing.

"Troop!" he called again. Conditioned like Pavlov's dogs, we came to attention at this command. We closed ranks, marched to the front of the drill hall, and listened to our last address as Corporal Wheeler spoke.

"Yeah, we know," he said. "But we're not telling anyone. Don't worry, ladies, your secret is safe with us. Your marching is just about the best we've ever seen on this base. Maybe not the best, but just about the best."

"It's the best," Don Withers interjected.

"Whatever." Wheeler smiled. "You'll be able to rehearse on your own now. You don't need me any more, but I'll be your leader during your Pass Out exercises. You have done well, gentlemen. I am proud to be your drill instructor, and you should all be proud of yourselves."

We were. Once again, our troop shared a common goal, a common ground, and a common emotion—pride.

"Yes, Corporal," we answered together. The drill hall went quiet as Francois sat at attention, tears flowing down his face. He alone did not know his future.

"Labeau?" Withers turned in his direction, then spoke in a voice we could all hear. "Constable Labeau, I have some news for you and your troop. The Force has decided to take your case on its own merits. Your doctor has been writing promising reports, and our Commanding Officer has recommended that you be allowed to graduate with your class. Your future, however, depends on you." Then Withers turned back to our troop. "Troop 18 will graduate with thirty-two recruits. Congratulations, gentlemen."

As one, we exploded into screams, yells, hurrahs, and cheers. All crowded around Francois and cheered again. Laughter mixed with tears; cheers mixed with sobs as we all tasted success.

"You're not following tradition today, you're making it." Don Withers repeated his friend's earlier comments.

More cheers, more tears, and more laughter.

Five minutes later we had resumed our troop formation as Francois wheeled his chair into place. Two rows of sixteen recruits lined up in exact formation in front of their instructors. Francois Labeau was once again truly and completely part of our troop.

"Caporals," Labeau said, proud for the first time since his accident, "Troop 18 tanks you for your help. We will make you proud next week."

Our instructors smiled. They were already proud.

Wheeler spoke. "I know you will, but one thing remains."

We waited, not knowing what "thing" remained.

"Tonight you have a date with destiny," he said. "Murder Ball. Do not fail."

Again, he knew our best-held secrets.

"With respect, Corporal, how did you know?" Outman asked.

Pointing up to the spectators' bleachers, Don Withers turned back toward our troop. "See that corner, way up at the back and to the left?" In the diffused daylight we looked in the direction of his finger. "Corporal Wheeler and I removed the corner lightbulb several months ago. It's dark here in the morning, and we've been sitting up there, in the corner of the parade hall, observing your progress for the past six months. During morning fatigue parade when Troop 19 refused to clean toilets, we were up there—in the shadows."

"And I'll bet you have been sitting in many odder places." Francois smiled as he added his comments, for it had become apparent that either Wheeler or Withers had been lurking on the other side of the elevator service room door while we wined and dined with Inspector Chicken.

"A few."

We laughed as Didarski, standing in the rear row, quietly made a chicken-clucking sound.

"Troop!" Wheeler shouted, and the troop snapped to attention.

"Tonight, do not fail. We're counting on you." His face grew serious. "Troop dismissed."

Troop 18 marched from the drill hall, tall and proud. For the first time, Francois did not follow the troop. He led it. And on the back of his wheelchair, someone had taped an aspirin.

Heads held high, we marched past the entrance to "C" block and turned left, into the mess. Another culinary experience.

"Dis is what give me de strength I need," Francois said, looking down at the lumps of fatty tissue on his plate. "I wonder how it is dat dey can make de vegetables so soft and de meat so crunchy?"

"It's not meat," Outman replied.

"Hey Francois, way to go, buddy. We're proud you're graduating with us," Burl called out.

"Yeah, Labeau, you're an ace," André added.

"That goes for me too, Frenchy. You got guts, man," I added.

Then from the adjoining table a deep voice interjected. "Yeah, Labeau, you got guts all right and I'll see them spilled on the dirt tonight." It was a Troop 19 mutant. He was sitting beside Smart Mouth.

"You tink you can do dat, scum-bucket? I'd slap your guts in de dirt, if you had any." Francois was practising Shita Wassa.

The temperature in the mess hall was rising as we stood to leave the table. If there was to be a fight, it would take place in the riding stable at nineteen hundred hours.

We would not fail.

A short wash and a shave, and our troop led the noon parade. Everyone shaved twice each day. It was the perfect thing to do. Five o'clock shadows were not allowed—not even at noon. Tourists watched as our troop marched by, keeping flawless time to the drummer. The other troops that followed marched rather well, but not as well as we did. Since our arrival, twelve more troops had formed up—approximately one troop every two weeks. The twelve troops that followed us were now our juniors. Troop 17 had graduated, and we led the parade. We were the senior troop.

We were the best.

Sadly, Francois still looked on from the sidewalk, but he wore his scarlet tunic as proudly as any member on the parade square. As our troop doubled around the square we almost lapped the junior troop from behind. Only two weeks into training, they marched like a flock of ducks on a hot waffle iron, and we tried not to smile. It reminded us of ourselves a short five and a half months earlier.

"Are they the prisoners?" one tourist asked his guide. My mind was thrown back to my arrival at Depot. That question had been asked about us and now my brain knew the answer: "Yes, they are the prisoners. Only after they learn to become a troop, a team, an individual troop that cares for itself as a whole more than any part ... only then will they cease to become prisoners." I remembered the lesson we had learned from Corporal Withers after our long confinement to barracks. He taught us to work as a team, a unit possessing one spirit.

Corporal Withers also taught us another great lesson, I thought. Having passed our last inspection, we received a visit later from Corporal Withers. He came to our barracks to offer unofficial congratulations, and he left us with the words "Uncommon freedom follows uncommon achievement."

Then our gaoler set us free with the simple words "Gentlemen, you are no longer prisoners."

I snapped out of my daydream as parade ended and the tourists left the square. We also departed to our next rehearsal—swimming.

In bathing suits, we stood on the cold concrete and prepared to enter the pool area. Corporal Thain, as usual, held the doors open for five minutes before giving us permission to enter.

"Troop, forward harch," he called, and we harched our cold feet and erect nipples onto the pool deck. More tourists lined the balcony and watched intently as we began our practice.

"Okay, ladies, line up on the north wall. Lumchuck, I want you to climb up the ladder, face the tourists, introduce yourself, then show them your best dive." We all remembered Larry's first fearful entry into the water. In these short five and a half months, he had progressed from his initial designation as "nonswimmer" to being awarded his Royal Lifesaving Bronze Medallion.

Confidently, he climbed the ladder and faced the crowd.

"My name is Constable Larry Lumchuck, ladies and gentlemen. I am a member of the Royal Canadian Mounted Police and a member of Troop 18." He stood poised on the edge of the platform, then jumped and plummeted headfirst into the water, barely making a ripple. Turning to the spectators sitting high in the bleachers, Corporal Thain declared, "Ladies and gentlemen, nearly six months ago, that man could not even swim, and look at him today."

The crowd leaned forward. A low rumble could be heard, then someone called out, "He's dead!"

We looked down at the bottom of the pool's deep end. Lumchuck remained motionless.

"He ain't freakin' dead," Corporal Thain replied. "He's just pretending. Aren't you, Lumchuck?"

Lumchuck remained motionless on the bottom, in fifteen feet of water.

"Aren't you, Lumchuck?"

No response. Larry's white body remained on the bottom.

Nearly a minute had elapsed and Corporal Thain showed concern.

"Bryant and Didarski," he said in low tones, "jump in there and get him out. This is a freakin' embarrassment."

"Can't, Corporal."

"Why not? I just ordered you to."

"He's swimming too fast."

Looking down into the water, we could see that Larry had begun his trek along the bottom of the pool. He did not surface until he had arrived at the shallow end.

"And that's how well we train a nonswimmer," Thain called out to the spectators, pretending the whole charade had been part of an elaborate plan.

Lumchuck climbed out of the pool and walked by Thain as he took his place in the troop. "You ever do that to me again and I'll personally rip your freakin' face off," said Thain.

"Yes, Corporal," Larry replied quietly.

The remainder of our swimming rehearsal went smoothly. We rescued drowning swimmers, retrieved ten-pound bricks from the bottom, and swam laps on top and beneath the surface of the water. Even Francois joined in. The water buoyed up his body, and using his impressive upper body strength, he not only swam with the best of us but developed a style that completely concealed his weak legs. His true rehearsal, however, would be during the evening, in the absence of our instructor. We had something special planned.

An old wooden chair had been placed in the showers, and as we helped Francois into his seat, Corporal Thain stood at the door, watching.

"You did okay, lads. Not freakin' good, but okay. I'm sure there'll be one or two parents that will enjoy your Pass Out." He smiled for the first time. "Maybe I'll have them check your shorts for tobacco stains? I think they'd be real proud of your hygiene." We laughed, then he added, "Oh, one more thing. Tonight ... tonight ..." He paused. "Don't freakin' lose."

Thain disappeared.

Everyone knew.

Everyone.

Troop 19 had become the scourge of Depot. Our instructors were counting on us to clean them up—and we would. Few would ever think that possible, but our training and our commitment would give us a strength that the junior troop could not yet muster. Besides, we had Francois—our hero—and we had something else: a plan.

Quickly we towelled off, donned gym shorts, and rehearsed our self-defence demonstration. André took the lead with a performance that surprised even Corporal Leitz. As with swimming, our rehearsal had been fine-tuned in the absence of our instructor.

Later we ate a light supper and returned to our dormitory to finalize and rehearse the plan that would neither follow nor set tradition. It would become a legend.

Everyone in the troop had a part in the attack against Troop 19.

The game was to be "sudden death." No rules and no time limit would be allowed. The game would end after the first goal was scored.

"This is the magic ball." André held up a football. Using white paint, he had painted "Troop 18" clearly on its side. "They'll never get this away from us—not unless they pry it from our bloodied, unconscious hands." We laughed, remembering our self-defence instructor's famous words.

"Outman, you got your knife?" André asked.

"In my sock."

"Good."

"Lumchuck, you got the extra ball?"

Larry reached into his oversized sweatshirt top and retrieved a half-inflated football he had carefully concealed. "Right here, Master," he said.

"Francois, you got that cane we carped from the post hospital?"

"I got dat," he answered, waving the dark wooden cane above his head. Then he slid it under his seat, concealing its entire length save for the handle, which protruded slightly between his legs. "It's kinda short, but I tink it'll take care of Smart Mouth."

"Good," André said. "Here's the plan one more time ..."

Nineteen hundred hours. We arrived ahead of Troop 19 and took our places against the north wall. André stood in front of the troop and Francois stood at the side.

"One last check," André called. "I take out the first three to make it to the centre, then ..."

"I run and fall on the ball, pull my knife and deflate it," Outman said.

"Then ..."

"Ball to Didarski, Didarski to Lumchuck, Lumchuck to Burl. Burl now has the Troop 18 ball. Teather falls down screaming he's broken his leg—Lumchuck goes crazy—Burl to Francois (secret pass). No one knows that Lumchuck has the second ball. Lumchuck throws the second ball in the air—Teather intercepts—then ..."

"Then we all pray." A large silhouette stood in the doorway. Seconds later it was joined by another, then another, and finally one more. It was Corporal Withers who had spoken, and he had been joined by Wheeler, Ribeault, and Thain. Ribeault carried with him a large first-aid kit.

"Then we all freakin'-well pray," Corporal Thain added.

The instructors took their places outside the riding arena in the darkness of a distant stable as Troop 19 entered from the opposite end.

"Rules are—" Didarksi began but was interrupted.

"You said no rules," the biggest of our adversaries in the other troop called out.

"Okay, just so we're in agreement."

"No rules!" they jeered.

"No rules," we agreed.

We were well equipped. Magazines had been taped to our shins under our sweatpants, and the toes of our hard black-leather ankle boots were cushioned with cotton batten, stolen or carped from the post hospital. With our shoes cushioned, we could kick harder without injuring our toes, and our ankle boots were somewhat better weapons than the running shoes worn by our enemies. Troop 19 wore running shoes, but Troop 18 had not planned to run. We had planned to fight.

Labeau carefully reached between his legs to ensure he could reach his cane in an emergency. We took our places behind our hockey nets, which sat in the sawdust and dirt.

Troop against troop.

Didarski walked out, showed the football to our opponents, and ensured that they saw, written in large white letters, the inscription "Troop 18."

"Sudden death. Winner takes all," he said, and held the ball high in the air before setting it down in the centre of the arena. Didarski returned to our troop. No one spoke.

Like sixty-four gunfighters facing off at the O.K. Corral, we stared into each other's eyes. Then a voice from the stables yelled, "Now!"

Everyone raced for the marked ball that Phil had placed in the centre of the arena. Bryant's legs exploded under him as he raced past the ball and flung himself though the air. Turning horizontal, he knocked three players over as Outman ran and fell on the ball. Quickly, Outman retrieved the small knife he had stowed in his sock and slashed the ball. Rolling on top of it, he squeezed the air out and flattened it. For a moment, no one knew where it was. Didarski reached down to help Outman to his feet while Don shoved the flat pigskin up under Phil's bulky sweatshirt. Didarski ran back toward our own net. Gracefully he grabbed Lumchuck and shoved the flat leather ball under Larry's shirt. A few seconds later, Burl collided head-on with Lumchuck and they both fell to the dirt. While I lay screaming that my leg was broken, Burl accepted the flat ball and stumbled to his feet. Burl feigned a serious leg injury and limped toward Francois. He stumbled as he approached the wheelchair and secretly passed the flat marked ball to Francois. Somewhere in the confusion, Lumchuck retrieved the second, new ball from under his sweatshirt, screamed insanely, and threw it carelessly in the air.

The remaining thirty seconds of the game will be recorded in Depot's history as the most underhanded and diabolical Murder Ball manoeuvre ever played.

While members of Troop 19 fumbled over their "unofficial" ball, Labeau slowly pushed his wheelchair through the dirt and lobbed the official marked ball into an unguarded net. Only one opponent challenged him. A quick strike to his knees by Francois' cane took care of the challenge.

Francois scored. The game he had started six months ago had finally come to an end. He had won!

"Score!" A voice came from the stable.

Instantly, all players stopped. Our troop stood beside our opponent's net, smiling and pointing to the flattened ball resting in their goal. It was clearly marked "Troop 18." The game ball.

"I don't know what you ladies are playing with down there, but it seems that our cripple has scored the only goal necessary."

"You used two balls. You slashed the play ball. That's cheating."

"You used a cripple," another voice added.

"Your game—your choice. No rules," André said, as he picked up the ball and threw it to Francois. "We win. You lose."

Troop 19 stood in silent shock as Francois added, "Seems like you guys got a lot of toilets to clean out. Tink you can do dat?"

We did not laugh at Troop 19. We had beaten them at their own game, and if they were ever to discover pride, it would be because they first saw it in our troop.

"Gentlemen," André addressed our vanquished foes, "seems like you lost. Remember this feeling when you're dealing with your junior troops. Pride and humility should both be worn carefully." Then he added, "With respect, gentlemen, don't ever call one of our troopmates a cripple again or we'll take you all to hell and leave you there. It has been a fine game. Perhaps we have all learned something." André looked at Labeau, then at Troop 19, then back at us. Our next move had also been planned. Slowly we walked toward them, shook their hands, and wished them well. As a reminder of our encounter, Francois handed over the slashed, flattened football as a trophy.

"We'll be at your graduation, fellahs. Good luck," said a voice at the back of their troop.

"Yeah. Good luck, guys," echoed another.

We left the arena and turned into the stable. Four shadowy figures lurked in the darkness, but we ignored them as we walked toward the exit.

"Good luck, Troop 18." The words came from the shadows. "Good luck."

Late that night we gathered for the last time in the room atop the elevator shaft. Each member of our troop was handed a freshly carped beer, and we toasted our success.

"To success."

"To Troop 19."

"To Wheeler and Withers."

"To beer."

"To Inspector Chicken, may he rest in peace."

"To the game."

"It's over," a soft voice added.

"It's over," we repeated.

"To us."

"To Troop 18."

"Ninjas all."

DEPOT DIVISION

The RCMP training academy, home of the "Mountie Makers" and the birthplace of Troop 18.

CHAPTER SIXTEEN
Pass Out—A Family Affair

Monday, April 1: I met my parents at the Regina airport on the last evening in March. The small airport was crowded with the thirty-two members of Troop 18, patiently awaiting the arrival of their friends and families. Airplanes arrived from the east and west, bringing a never-ending assortment of mothers, fathers, sisters, brothers, and girlfriends. It was a tradition to invite those you loved to your graduation, in order to show them what you had learned and who you had become. The tradition had existed for many years—and it would continue for many more.

Phil stood beside me, and Don was beside him.

"Hey, Prairie Dog," I called. "How come your folks are flying in? They live pretty close, don't they?"

"Dad's not up to driving," he said. "Besides, they came to see my graduation, not a couple of hundred miles of flat prairie road. How's about you, Phil?" he asked.

"Yeah. Folks should be here on the next flight. They'll be tired. Halifax is a long ways to fly." Phil looked sad.

"Something still eating at you, isn't it?" André said.

"Yeah." He looked at the floor.

"Your girlfriend?"

"Yeah." Phil choked out a short response.

"She gonna marry that lawyer guy she left you for?"

"That's the word I hear."

"Hey, you got folks coming. You should be happy."

"What about you, André?"

"No folks."

"What are you doing here?"

"Maybe somebody'll adopt me."

Half an hour later Phil Didarski greeted his parents. They met, they embraced, and Phil's mother cried. Her son had grown up. As André watched, their gaze turned toward him, and Phil motioned André to join them. No one knew what was said between the four of them, but five minutes later Mr. and Mrs. Didarski left the airport with Phil and their newly adopted son, André Bryant. In small groups, parents left the airport with their sons and were taken to their waiting hotel rooms. Tonight everyone would sit up late listening to tales told by their sons, and tomorrow they would watch those sons graduate. Mr. and Mrs. Didarski would watch with pride as two sons graduated.

My parents arrived from Ontario later in the evening, and I took them to their hotel room. We sat together and talked well past midnight. We shared private words and thoughts. Very private.

The next morning, as the scratchy sound of reveille played over the loudspeakers, Troop 18 rose to prepare for the day.

It was a quiet morning. The usual banter was missing and some of the excitement had left the air.

"Folks said I've changed," Don Outman said while shaving.

"Mine too," Harold called out from the showers.

"Same here," Phil added.

They were right. We had all changed, and from that day forth, our relationships with our parents would be different. Some relationships would be better, some worse, but all would be different.

That morning we were excused from early morning parade and fatigues, and as we looked out the window, we smiled.

"Troop 19 Riiight Marker. Presenting our troop for toilet swabbing!" a husky voice called out. Troop 19 was now officially a "senior" troop, yet it was volunteering for toilet duties.

"Looks like we did some good." André pressed his face against the window. "They're leading the way, volunteering to perform the dirtiest of chores on the base."

"I wonder why dey are doing dat?" Francois pulled himself out of his wheelchair and supported his body against the window sill.

"There is dignity in work, when the work is freely accepted," André said. "Looks like one game of Murder Ball and the respect we showed for them gave them some dignity."

One game of Murder Ball had produced the best troop of toilet swabbers Depot had ever seen. Even more important, it had created something more valuable to the RCMP: An individual troop—Troop 19.

The serious mood we had shared as we thought about the changes our parents had perceived in us began to fade, and conversations became light and cheery as we dressed for breakfast. Proudly, we prepared our dormitory for inspection by both NCOs and parents, then left our barracks to meet our families for pancakes and bacon.

Zero eight hundred hours. On this day, our parents were asked to join their sons for breakfast at the mess. Countless letters home containing complaints about our food would be validated.

Pushing our trays along the stainless-steel rails, we watched and listened in shock as we approached the food bins. Behind the glass, our cook was wearing a clean apron and he cheerfully called out, "Eggs, ladies and gentlemen. Scrambled, fried, or cooked to order. Pan-fried hash browns and your choice of side bacon, back bacon, or link sausages. Condiments include any choice you like. Perhaps freshly prepared applesauce? Please help yourself to your choice of beverages. We have coffee, tea, or fresh apple, grapefruit, or orange juice. For dessert we have fresh fruit or waffles and your choice of preserves."

The pancakes were missing!

It was inconceivable that such a change could have taken place. One hour earlier, the more junior troops had dined at the mess, but they would not be treated as human until their graduation. By straining, we could see farther into the kitchen, where a large garbage pail still held the remnants of the first breakfast service. The trash can was half-filled with pancakes and strips of greasy, half-cooked pork belly.

"I don't know what you've been complaining about, son," my dad said through two cheeks swollen with hash browns and sausage. "This seems like pretty good food to me."

"But we are just hoping dat dey don't serve jello," Francois said as we all laughed.

After their fine meal, our parents were escorted on a tour of the base that included a service at the chapel and a visit to the museum. Their tour ended a short time later—at the freakin' swimming pool.

Corporal Thain stood poised with his eight-foot bamboo cane, and he looked up and spoke to our parents in the balcony.

"Ladies and gentlemen, you have before you the best freakin' troop I have ever had the pleasure to instruct. Many of them came here as nonswimmers but under my careful instruction and the guidance of this fine cane, they have all earned their Royal Lifesaving Bronze Medallion. I would now like to demonstrate their lifesaving skills and swimming ability.

"Lumchuck, front and centre," he called. We had practised our swimming drill, and Thain had no idea of the plan that was about to unfold.

"Mr. and Mrs. Lumchuck, your son could not swim when he came here. That was a freakin' shame, but I would like you to observe his progress now." Turning toward Larry, he said softly, "Make it freakin' good, lad."

"Yes, Corporal," Larry called out loudly.

As Lumchuck climbed the ladder to the high platform, Corporal Thain narrated. "Your son, Mr. and Mrs. Lumchuck, will now execute the most graceful dive this pool has ever seen. Having entered the water without so much as a ripple, he will swim underwater to the far end of the pool. There, he will retrieve a ten-pound brick, surface, and return the brick to the deep end."

Larry stood proudly on the edge of the platform, and we watched as his toes curled over the edge. His mother had defeated her cancer—for now—and her pride in her son's success was evident. She had a new son and Larry had a new mother.

"Make dis a good one," Francois said quietly.

Larry turned toward his parents, nodded, and returned his gaze to the water below. Then he dove.

His body was flung, sprawling and twisting, from the platform, and a gasp could be heard as he plummeted fifteen feet to meet the water's surface. Lumchuck smacked down hard with the loudest and most painful belly flop recorded in the history of Depot.

Thain stood motionless, barely speaking the words "freakin' horrible."

Instantly upon hitting the water, Larry's body sank to the bottom, where he remained motionless, while Corporal Thain decided what to do next. We did not give him the opportunity to make a decision.

Our parents had risen to their feet and crowded to the edge of the wrought-iron railing. Mrs. Lumchuck's face was frozen in shock. We had rehearsed this many times in private, and our plan was about to unfold.

"I can do dis," Francois said as he pushed himself from the wheelchair and threw himself into the water. Using only his arms, he swam along the surface until he was directly above Larry's motionless shape. Taking in a lung full of air, he dove to the bottom of the pool and pulled Larry's limp body to the surface. Once there, Francois rolled the "victim" onto his back and began towing him toward the edge of the pool. Realizing the whole charade had been planned, everyone laughed.

Even Corporal Thain.

Having towed his victim to the shallow end, Francois reached down and retrieved the ten-pound brick. Lumchuck placed the brick on his chest and Labeau continued to tow his happy victim back to the deep end of the pool. Lumchuck was secretly holding onto Francois' legs while his rescuer used both arms to propel them through the water. Upon reaching the pool's edge, Francois waved to the audience and said, "And dat, ladies and gentlemen, is how we save a life." The assembly of parents exploded into applause as we wheeled Francois' chair to the edge of the pool. Unaided, Francois climbed out of the pool and into his chair.

Together, the Lumchucks and Labeaus led the cheering and applause, which went on for several minutes. Each time it started to die down, someone would rekindle the flame and the cycle would begin again. With cheers, tears, and laughter, the parents expressed their pride in what their sons had become.

A few more demonstrations completed the one-hour presentation, and as we left for the showers a standing ovation signalled our success and heralded our departure from the freakin' swimming pool.

While we changed for our next demonstration, Corporal Thain continued to tell our parents how good his instruction had been and how freakin' good we had become. He did not, however, lecture them on the topic of hygiene.

Self-defence was next. Bleachers had been carefully set out by Troop 19 for our parents.

Corporal Leitz faced the benches as he spoke. "Ladies and gentlemen, six months ago your sons came to my gymnasium uncoordinated, weak, and lacking self-confidence. Today they are men, capable of defending not only themselves, but you and all Canadian citizens whom they have sworn to protect." We watched as our parents took in every word. "I have not taught them to fight clean. I have not given them any rules of engagement. I have taught them to fight hard and win." As Leitz raised his voice, we watched our parents flinch. "Losing is not an option!"

After Leitz's words finished echoing off the walls, he continued, "First we will demonstrate a manoeuvre called a breakfall. It is designed to allow a man to take a fall without being hurt. Didarski, front and centre!"

Phil snapped to attention, ran ten steps, cleared a five-foot high-jump bar, and landed on his face—a performance reminiscent of Lumchuck's belly flop.

SMACK!

The sound of flesh on half-inch-thick rubber mats drew a gasp from our parents. Phil's motionless body remained on the mat.

"As you can see, this recruit has just dropped from a height of five feet and he has not hurt himself. Have you, Didarski?"

Springing to his feet and standing at attention, Phil called out, "No, Corporal." His face, forearms, and hands, however, had already begun to turn red from the hard slap on the shiny mats.

"Take your place."

"Yes, Corporal." Phil returned to the troop as our parents applauded.

Various members of our troop were called to demonstrate kicks, punches, and blocks. Although the "fights" had been rehearsed, we continued to impress our parents with moves that looked spontaneous but had been planned with the precision of a Las Vegas dance chorus line. Everything had been staged—everything except Don Outman's handling of Harold Burl. Realizing that Harold was a poor actor, Don applied the carotid control hold as it should be applied. Firmly. "It is a simple matter of restricting the blood to the brain, folks," Don said. "Then our assailant will gently sleep and nobody gets hurt." After holding the pressure on Harold's neck for fifteen seconds, he carefully laid his twitching body on the mats. Twenty seconds later, Harold opened his eyes, stood up, and performed a very wobbly bow to the wide-eyed parents.

More applause.

Francois watched our demonstrations. Sitting tall in his wheelchair, he was as proud of us as we were of him.

"Your sons have been taught to take every advantage in a fight, to always win, and to always be prepared," Leitz said to the parents as he walked backwards toward the wall. "You will have no worries." Leitz turned to our troop, winked, then returned his gaze to our parents.

"This troop has also taught me something very important. It is a skill that I think we shall include in our self-defence training some day, but until then, perhaps a simple demonstration would be in order. Please understand, folks, that this has not been rehearsed."

We wondered what Leitz had planned.

"Outman, front and centre." Don jumped to attention, marched to the centre of the gymnasium, and faced Corporal Leitz.

"Outman," Leitz shouted, "you are faced with the best fighter in the world. Me! I am about to take you apart limb from limb. Your nearest backup is an hour away and you must act. You have three seconds before I begin to administer the beating of your life. What are you going to do?"

Don was in shock. He didn't know how to react. Then, from the rear of the troop, came a faint voice. "Shita Wassa."

"C'mon, dirtball, you wanna dance, c'mon take your best freakin' shot, puke!" Don screamed. "I said c'mon, scum-bucket." Our parents sat in shock, not knowing what would happen. "But before you do, take a good luck at this face. It gets into a fight at least once each week. That's over fifty each year, and in five years you're looking at a face that's been in over 250 fights! You see any marks on this face? Do you, slimeball?" Don pointed to his face. "That's 'cause there ain't any. I've taken on bigger pukes than you before breakfast, so why not now." Saliva flew from his lips and his face turned red as he continued his barrage. "C'mon, c'mon, c'mon!" Don screamed at the top of his lungs. "I'm crazy, okay? I got charged with attempted murder just last week when I pulled a man's eyes out and turned them around backwards, just so he could watch himself die. So you wanna dance ... do you, dirtball?"

"Constable!" Leitz screamed, and Don snapped to attention. "Ladies and gentlemen, even when faced with insurmountable odds, a police officer cannot back down. This is how your sons will face their assailants. Even if they should fail, they will not fail while retreating."

Don returned to his place in the troop amidst cheers and laughter. As the applause died down, an older man's voice could be heard saying, "That's my son."

Leitz appeared pleased with our performance as he motioned a colleague forward. "I will now turn this class over to Corporal Steel, Troop 18's physical education instructor."

"Parents, family, and loved ones, I would like to take this opportunity to introduce you to the members of Troop 18," Steel announced loudly and confidently. "As I call their names, they will present themselves to you. Constable Lumchuck."

Larry took two steps forward and stood at attention.

"Constable Lumchuck was a bowling ball when he arrived here. He was so fat that if he fell on his face, he'd rock himself to sleep trying to get back up." Everyone laughed except Larry's parents. They sat in shock, although still proud of their son's new body. Steel continued. "Constable Lumchuck has lost over forty pounds and has gained strength beyond even my belief. Lumchuck, climb that rope."

In the centre of the gym, a two-inch-thick hemp rope hung from the twenty-foot-high ceiling. Larry approached the rope and began to climb it.

"Now what is interesting, ladies and gentlemen, is that Constable Lumchuck will continue the climb using only his hands."

Taking the command from Corporal Steel, Larry thrust his legs out horizontally and climbed to the ceiling. He had practised this many times, but never without the use of his legs. On the way down he faltered and slid the last three feet to the floor, but no one noticed.

Except Steel.

"Thank you, Lumchuck. Well done, lad." Neither one acknowledged the painful wounds to Larry's hands. This day, nothing would detract from perfection.

Larry took his place with the troop, holding his hands closed so no one would see the blood.

"Perhaps one of the finest recruits to grace this gymnasium is an individual whom I have watched closely for the past six months." Corporal Steel's throat tightened as he spoke. "He is, without doubt, one of the strongest in body and spirit that I have ever met, and I would like you all to witness the power of this young man who would not quit."

Turning to the troop, Steel called, "Labeau."

As prearranged, two members of the troop lifted an iron bar mounted with 200 pounds of weight. Carefully they rested it on the arms of Francois' wheelchair.

Francois gripped the bar, and without any expression on his face, he lifted it over his head. All parents cheered as Francois' parents stared at their son.

Steel kept talking to the audience while Francois continued his repetitions, resting only a few seconds between lifts. No one heard what Corporal Steel had to say until Francois had finished demonstrating his feat of strength.

"... and once again, I say to you, proudly, I present the members of Troop 18, police officers who can run farther, lift more, and climb higher than anyone on this base."

Then he added an engaging smile and said, "You may applaud, if you like."

Each member of our troop had demonstrated a feat of strength or endurance or a mastery of self-defence. Phil's face was still red from the strike on the mats. Larry's closed hands still hid the skin

THE FINAL CEREMONY

Standing at attention, the troop watches as one of the members receives his badge. This is the day we had all worked for—our success was measured by one small piece of metal and the pride that came with it.

that had peeled away from his palms, and Francois' arms still trembled. He had broken his own record.

We showered and returned to barracks to prepare for afternoon parade. Meanwhile, our parents were treated to a second meal at the Road Kill Cafe. Unfortunately, we would miss that meal.

For their sons, leather was more important than food.

"Paaarade aaatenshuun!" Corporal Wheeler screamed. Noon-day parade was called to attention, and our parents and girlfriends watched intently.

Troop 18 headed the parade and we stood taller and more erect than we had ever stood in the preceding six months. Don Outman hid his devilish prairie-dog smile, Larry Lumchuck sucked his stomach in until he could hardly breathe, and Phil Didarski fought, successfully, the aerodynamic pull on his left ear that had always caused him to veer off course.

As the troops continued their march around the parade square, Wheeler spoke to our parents.

"Ladies and gentlemen, we will break off Troop 18 and march them over to the drill hall for a small demonstration."

"Troop 18, right wheel—parade left wheel." With those two commands, we were surgically removed from the parade. "Troop 18 proceed to the drill hall and assume your positions," Wheeler called. At the drill hall, our parents would be privy to a sampling of the discipline and humiliation their sons had undergone for six months.

Once inside the hall, our troop split into groups and waited for the arrival of our audience. Five minutes later, the spectators, led by Corporal Wheeler, stood waiting. "Ladies and gentlemen, I would like to introduce you to Troop 18 as they existed just three months ago." Corporal Wheeler walked to the east wall and stopped a few feet from a full-length mirror. Larry Lumchuck stood at attention, both feet firmly planted in a waist-high garbage can and the metal garbage can lid on his head. Facing the mirror, he continued saluting himself every fifteen seconds while calling out his own self-administered reprimand: "My name's Donald Duck and I walk like one, too."

Corporal Wheeler explained. "Lumchuck had a problem for the first three months. He could not distinguish his right leg from his left. We fixed that problem." He turned to Lumchuck. "Didn't we, lad?"

"Quack, quack, quack," Larry replied.

"Good. Now on to our next problem." Nearby, Phil Didarski walked in endless clockwise circles. "Constable Didarski has this aerodynamic disability. It seems, Mr. and Mrs. Didarski, that your son was born with an oversized left ear." Phil's parents smiled. "In order to overcome this tragedy, we had to strengthen the right side of his body so that he could walk in a straight line. Seems to have worked quite well, doesn't it, Constable Didarski?"

"Yes, Corporal."

Corporal Wheeler continued. "And then there's the punishment for any dozy little man who cannot come to attention properly." He smiled. "Outman. Aaatenshuun!" Don came to a sloppy state of alertness. "Outman, I see you still haven't learned. You're so uncoordinated that you can't walk while I chew gum." Don pretended not to smile. "Would you please execute the required manoeuvre. I think that lady would be just fine." Wheeler pointed to a young girl in the crowd. It was Don's younger sister. Marching over to his sister, Don snapped perfectly to attention and called out loudly enough for the entire audience to hear, "My name is Mickey Mouse. I have large feet. Would you have supper with me tonight?"

His sister blushed and then giggled. "Sure, Don. I'd like that," she answered. Don saluted his sister, winked, then returned to the troop.

The demonstration blended humiliation with discipline and continued for another ten minutes. As we glanced into the crowd, we could sense an understanding developing. Our folks began to comprehend our drill instructor's methods and the discipline that had been distilled in their sons.

"Troop 18, close ranks!" Corporal Wheeler screamed so hard we expected to see both lungs spew from his mouth.

"Eeeyes left!" Our heads jerked to the left as we shuffled our feet, ensuring our shoulders were four inches apart.

Four inches precisely.

GRADUATION:
A FAMILY AFFAIR

Mothers, fathers, family and girlfriends were invited to be a part of the graduation ceremonies. It was a time of pride for all recruits, the successful completion of six months of blood, sweat, and tears—and camaraderie.

"Eeeyes front!" Like a synchronized machine our heads jerked forward. Our parents looked on, not knowing what was next.

"Troop 18, fooorwaaard harch!" Sounding like one giant marching Mountie, we began to march forward, toward our parents. Their eyes grew large as we approached, and it seemed for an instant that we would continue until we had crushed them against the wall.

"Please. Stay where you are," Wheeler ordered the audience as we closed the distance. Only inches away, he called out his final order. "Troop 18, halt!" Slamming our feet into the floor we stopped—nearly touching the front line of parents. Staring straight ahead we stood at attention, not even acknowledging their presence. "Troop aaabout face!" We spun on one foot and completed a 180-degree turn.

"Fooorwaaard harch," Wheeler called out, a bit softer.

We flawlessly performed the manoeuvres we had practised. The troop turned right, left, and reversed our direction on command from Corporal Wheeler. After fifteen minutes of precision drill, the troop was called to attention.

"Ladies and gentlemen, we have one additional manoeuvre we would like to demonstrate." Slamming his leg into the drill hall floor, Corporal Wheeler's face took on a granite-like façade as he ordered the troop into motion, "Troop 18, fooorwaaard harch!"

There were no more commands, and only the sounds of our boots striking the floor filled the hall. Troop 18 wheeled and marched from corner to corner as we executed patterns that delighted, amazed, and amused our audience. At the end of the silent demonstration, the troop marched in formation up to Corporal Wheeler. Only inches away, we stopped.

"Troop 18 dismissed!" he screamed. For the last time, sputum flew from his mouth and landed on our faces and scarlet tunics.

Upon command, the troop turned left, took one step forward, and broke ranks. We approached our parents, embraced, and walked away to our own private space in the drill hall, where we would talk.

As I spoke to my mother and father, my eye caught a lone figure sitting high in the corner of the drill hall observation deck. Instantly I knew it was Corporal Don Withers. Surveying the hall, my eyes met with Lumchuck, Didarski, and André, then Francois. They too had felt the silent presence of our teacher, sitting in the shadows. He had come to watch our graduation. He was as proud of us as anyone in the hall.

He had become our friend.

We were given the next three hours to spend with our parents. As was the custom, we took them on our own tour of Depot, showing them things they had not seen on their organized tour. In turn, all parents were shown the monument erected to commemorate members who had been killed on duty, the graveyard, the clean toilets, and, yes, even the burial place of Inspector Chicken.

No parents, however, were shown the location of our secret dining hall atop the elevator shaft. That was to be kept above all secrets, for it was a Ninja secret.

Later I learned that we all talked with our parents during those three hours in a manner never before tried. We were adults now, and we spoke like adults, not children. Even so, none of us truly shared all our feelings with our parents. Our fears of failure, our internal fights, and our homesickness were items to be talked about in the days to come. But today we graduated—Passed Out—and our pride overshadowed everything.

After the tour, we left our parents to prepare for dinner and our graduation ceremony.

We had succeeded.

Ninjas all!

> "Courage is not merely the greatest of human virtues,
> but the first. Without courage, no other virtues would
> exist."
>
> Corporal Wheeler, Drill Instructor

CHAPTER SEVENTEEN
Graduation—One Last Murder Ball,
One Last Chicken

Monday evening, April 1: Graduation exercises were finished, and a formal supper had been planned in the drill hall. At the official ceremonies to be conducted following supper, we would be presented with our badges and police identification cards.

Six o'clock in the evening: Troop 19 had prepared the drill hall for our graduation supper. Tables were covered with crisp white tablecloths and were precisely set out in a uniform pattern. The main table was adorned with souvenirs, reminders of our six-month training period.

Parents, sons, family members, and instructors had taken their seats, patiently waiting for the ceremonies to commence. As was the custom, the junior troop served the dinner, which was superb. No longer were we to be assaulted with mystery meat and jello surprise. Tonight we would dine on real food.

Chicken!

Immediately after supper, our junior troop honoured us with a few well-placed comments and gifts.

"Ladies and gentlemen," a designated member of Troop 19 called out, "on this table you can see many artifacts and mementos of your sons' Depot experience: Aspirins to ease their pain, brass polish, which they have applied to every doorknob on this base, remnants of plaster casts used to immobilize sprains and broken bones, and even a spray bottle of vinegar, which I am sure they have already told you about." Everyone laughed. "But under this silver dome before me lies something that our troop has come to hold most dear to our heart."

The silver dome was raised, and sitting alone on the platter for all to see was a slashed, flattened, dirty football. It was clearly marked in white paint with the words "Troop 18."

"Troop 18, we salute you," he said, and cheers from our servants shook the walls and rattled the wine glasses.

The cheering subsided. Our parents had already been told the story of our first and our last Murder Ball game.

"Good luck, gentlemen," our junior troop called out in unison.

Then the room grew quiet in anticipation as Corporal Don Withers approached the head table and stood by the podium. Every member of Troop 18 rose and applauded as their hero faced the gathering. Withers motioned us back into our chairs and spoke. "I have been asked by the men of Troop 18 to address you tonight," he said, looking not at the scarlet tunics, but at the parents. Don looked impressive. His waist was trim, his scarlet tunic impeccably pressed, and his leather rivalled Corporal Wheeler's.

"I will be brief," he continued. "Ladies and gentlemen, today you have watched your sons in action. You have seen what they can do and what they have become. The Royal Canadian Mounted Police is often referred to as 'Canada's Finest,' but I am not sure that is true."

Withers' words shocked us. For six months we had been trained to believe we were the best police force in Canada—perhaps the best in the world.

"No, I cannot guarantee any of you that your sons are the best in Canada. Maybe they are, maybe they aren't." He took a moment to survey the room. "One thing I can assure you all—and I would like you to remember my words, please." All eyes were on Don Withers as he continued, "Your sons have become the best we can make them, and they have grown to be the best men they know how to become. No one could ask more."

We were humbled by his words.

Corporal Withers raised a glass of wine in a toast. "To Troop 18," he said.

Everyone stood. "To Troop 18," the chorus responded.

During the speeches, Troop 19 had quietly set a long table beside a small podium and covered it with a horse blanket. On this traditional shadrak our badges and identification cards had been placed.

After the last toast, our Commanding Officer, Assistant Commissioner Holmes, took his place behind the podium and commanded: "Troop!"

Quickly we stood, left our tables, and took up our formation before our Commanding Officer and corporals Withers and Wheeler. Corps Sergeant Major Bilby stood behind the table. Once we had been queued by our Commanding Officer, Bilby would hand the badges and cards to Assistant Commissioner Holmes for presentation.

In alphabetical order, our names were called.

Individually we broke ranks, marched to the podium, saluted our Commanding Officer, and accepted our badge and identification. Saluting once again, we then returned to our troop.

All troopmates had received their badges ... except one.

Francois.

"Mr. Labeau, if you would please come to the podium, we have a special duty for you to perform here tonight." Corporal Wheeler spoke the words clearly for everyone to hear.

"I tink dat is me you are wanting?" Francois' father spoke up. His strong French accent caused us to smile. He sounded just like his son.

"Yes, sir. That is you," Wheeler replied. "If you would please come here for a moment, we have one more duty to perform."

Unsure of himself, Mr. Labeau approached the podium as our Commanding Officer spoke. "Ladies and gentlemen, we have a special function to perform this evening, and it is my pleasure to turn these proceedings over to Corporal Wheeler, your instruct—er—your sons' drill instructor. Corporal Wheeler, if you please."

Wheeler took a step forward as he accepted a solitary badge and identification card in a brown leather case. "Mr. Labeau, if you please?" He handed the case to Francois' father, who stood beside him.

"Ladies and gentlemen, I am sure you have all heard of Francois' story from your sons. You all know of his injury, how close he came to death, and you all know of the remarkable recovery he has made." Heads nodded in agreement. "Francois will not be leaving Depot for another month or two, but he will be officially graduating with his troop." Smiles sprang up throughout the room. "On permission from our Commanding Officer, we have reserved this final presentation to be made to the member of Troop 18 who has shown us all that courage is not merely the greatest of human virtues, but the first. Without courage, no other virtues would exist." The room remained silent. "It is because of the incredible courage shown by Constable Labeau that this presentation is possible." Mrs. Labeau sat proudly, watching the ceremony unfold.

"Constable Labeau!" Wheeler said. Don Outman began to push Francois' wheelchair forward.

"No," Francois whispered. "No, I can do dis."

Our entire formation held its breath. Slowly, shakily, Francois pushed himself up. In an eternity that probably only lasted a few seconds, he pulled down at the tails of his scarlet tunic and adjusted his gunbelt.

"Focus, Francois—focus," we heard André whisper from behind.

Slowly Francois took a step. Then another. Then another. One foot short of the podium, he stopped and stood, staring straight ahead. Legend would have it that he stood straighter than any recruit had ever stood during graduation ceremonies.

"Constable Labeau," Wheeler broke the awe-filled silence, "I congratulate you, sir, on your spirit, your strength and your ..." Wheeler's voice faltered. "... and your courage," he continued. "Today you have graduated, and we are all so very proud of you." Then, turning to Francois' father, he went on, "Mr. Labeau, six months ago your boy left home and today I would like to present to you a man I have grown to respect. You may now present him with his badge."

No one in the drill hall could see clearly. Mothers had taken out tissues and hankies, and fathers were pretending not to cry.

"Mr. Labeau, I present to you, Constable Francois Labeau."

Mr. Labeau handed Francois the small leather case and embraced his son in front of everyone.

AND THE TRADITION
CARRIES ON ...

Constable Brian Powell carries on the tradition first established in 1873. Like all modern Mounties, he must embrace the same code of conduct instilled in Troop 18 three decades ago. Here, he is seen wearing his Medal of Bravery, which he received after crashing through a large window to carry a person out of a burning house.

To all modern Mounties I pass on the advice given to our troop by Corporal Don Withers. "Make your decisions based on what is ethical ... not on what you fear will bring punishment or praise, but what you deem to be noble and just."

Francois smiled as the tears ran down his face. Turning toward our Commanding Officer, he saluted. His salute was returned.

Then Francois made a move that was totally unrehearsed and unauthorized. He saluted his father.

"Do you tink I am a man, fodder?" he whispered.

"Yes, my son, I tink you are."

The drill hall exploded into cheers as Francois slowly made his way back to his wheelchair. Mothers, fathers, and troopmates cheered for the man who walked unsteadily back to his wheelchair and sat down.

Each member of Troop 18 had reflected on the small symbol that gave Francois his inner strength. As he walked, unsteady on his feet, only we could see our secret.

On Francois' back, taped to the leather cross-strap of his gunbelt, was a small white object. André had taped it there just prior to our graduation dinner.

An aspirin.

Francois settled into his chair and our troop was whole again.

Then our Commanding Officer stepped forward, saluted our troop, turned toward our parents, and stated: "This graduation ceremony is now concluded."

PARADE SQUARE

The parade square sits quietly, holding secret its memories of our troop and patiently waiting for the next "individual troop" to stand on its surface and "FORWARD HARCH!"

"Farewells are necessary before good friends can meet again."

Richard Bach

CHAPTER EIGHTEEN
Departure—Four More Quarts of Oil

Wednesday, April 2: The day following our graduation ceremony was a day of goodbyes. We talked with our families about our training and what it meant to us. Later, we all said goodbye as they boarded their airplanes and flew home. After saying our farewells to our parents, we prepared ourselves to depart for our new homes.

As my parents' flight headed east to Ontario, my mind turned west to my first posting—Vancouver, British Columbia.

The prairie weather had risen to a balmy 45 degrees Fahrenheit as I loaded my few worldly possessions back into my 1958 Dodge. The note my father had attached to the rearview mirror a lifetime ago was still there. "Add a quart of oil every four hundred miles," it said. I smiled and added yet another piece of tape to hold it in place.

As I finished loading my car, I realized that our troop had formed up for the last time. Awkwardly, and once again unsure of ourselves, we assembled in the parking lot to say goodbye.

"'Bye, Prairie Dog, I'll miss you."

"'Bye, Phil. Get that ear fixed, eh?"

"'Bye, Krzyszyk. Did I pronounce it okay this time?"

"'Bye, Larry. Keep the weight off."

"'Bye, André. Hope you find a home."

"'Bye, Harold. Don't worry so much."

"'Bye, Francois. *Bonne chance, mon ami*. Good luck, my friend."

I drove away from the parking lot slowly. I could not look back on my friends ... my troopmates ... my brothers. Saying goodbye was painful.

It had been six months of hell, punctuated with achievement and camaraderie that is not found in the common hour. It had been "the best of times and the worst of times."

In only six months, our minds and bodies had changed. Some would say our youth had died, but it would be more accurate to say

EPILOGUE

It is now more than thirty years later and I am contemplating a new challenge—retirement.

As I look back, I feel a sense of mystery and longing. I have no way of knowing the fate of all my troopmates. The RCMP keeps track only of serving members, not of those who have retired.

I can share with you, however, the fates (or partial fates) of a few of my troopmates.

DON OUTMAN (Prairie Dog) was transferred to Vancouver International Airport. Five years later, he left the Force to return to his farm and his family. He married a prairie girl and, I am told, lived happily ever after. Don never shot another gopher.

HAROLD BURL was transferred to a small detachment in Saskatchewan, and he was medically discharged within the year. Harold worried too much.

PHIL DIDARSKI was transferred to Prince Edward Island. He served a full career and has recently taken his pension. Yes, he did meet another girl and fall madly in love. Their three children and a lasting marriage are a testament to their love.

KEN KRZYSZYK was transferred to New Brunswick and enjoyed a long, successful career. He finally married, in his mid-thirties. He and his wife had two children. Ken retired shortly after completing twenty-five years of service.

FRANCOIS LABEAU was transferred to Regina detachment, and after serving on "light duties" in an administrative capacity for six months, he was transferred to his home province of Quebec. His recovery was complete. Francois' career was a very successful one, but will remain confidential.

ANDRÉ BRYANT was transferred to Ontario. The following year he left the Force. His present whereabouts are unknown. André remains a mystery. He rarely spoke of his past and never shared his future plans with any troopmates. He was a wise and gentle man, and I hope that some day our paths will again cross. Until then, André, if you are reading this, I hope you have found a home.

As for me, I am sitting here at this keyboard, wondering if you liked our story ...

that parts of us had been reshaped. The part of us that was childish and uncertain had been purged by our instructors. We no longer doubted ourselves or dwelled on our weaknesses. Instead, we had built on our strengths. We had learned that courage was not the absence of fear, but rather the mastery of it.

Earlier than most, we were brought face to face with the confused values of the '60s generation. Drugs were not part of our culture, and "the child within" was put aside. If we were to perform our duty, our strength would come from "the adult within."

Depot Division, home of the Mountie Makers, had completed its task successfully.

As I drove west, Corporal Wheeler became but a memory along with my other instructors. They would all serve out their tour of duty and move on to other successful postings during the following year. Except for Don Withers. He died shortly after completing his tour of duty as instructor.

"'Bye, Don. Thanks. Happy trails, my friend. I will never forget you."

On the Trans-Canada Highway, I pulled over just five miles west of Regina's city limits and parked. I was leaving Depot. I was reminded of that morning, six months earlier, when I had left home. I wondered if the child I was then would have been proud of the man I had become. Looking up at the white fluffy clouds that hung in the clean sky, I conjured the faces of my troopmates and my instructors, each again smiling and saying goodbye.

I thought back to when I said goodbye to my childhood friend, Ben. Like Ben, I felt that I was going home. To a new home. "Goodbye, Ben. I miss you, buddy."

Goodbyes are necessary before friends can meet again. The pain of departure was gone now, and I smiled back at the clouds. Leaving Regina, I was taking with me memories and experiences that had made me strong and would stay with me forever.

Four cans of motor oil rattled on the back floor of my car as I accelerated onto the blacktop and drove off into the west.

For six months of my life, I had been spit upon, shouted at, beaten, starved, and humiliated.

Boy, those were the good ol' days.